Praise for Drops of Wisdom

"I've known Rick Moss for almost 50 years as a friend and a fellow traveler on the path to awakening. He has always been a source of inspiration to me, and the knowledge and tools he's shared that have so profoundly enhanced my life, he is now sharing with you in this remarkable book.

Using his profound intuitive ability, his Drops of Wisdom flow with grace and authenticity. He thoughtfully explores topics like Great-Love, Relationships, Stillness, and Healing the Hurt Child Within and offers exercises in each chapter that will support you in implementing the knowledge in your day-to-day life. Any one of these processes can facilitate a dramatic shift.

I also love the quotes he's chosen. They add additional depth and power to his teachings.

But perhaps more than anything else, I can feel and hear a Divine Presence behind his words--a presence that will profoundly help us all to heal and grow."

~ **Debra Poneman**, International Speaker, Bestselling Author and Founder of Yes to Success, Inc.

"I found this book to be more than a collection of wise sayings. It is a user's guide to deepening and enriching one's way of loving. We find out how to move from ego attachment as love to unconditional higher self-giving as love. We then parent ourselves and come to love ourselves with the heart of God."

~ **David Richo**, Psychotherapist, teacher, writer, and workshop leader. Author of *Triggers, How to Be an Adult in Relationships,* and *The Five Things We Cannot Change.*

"I'm overwhelmed by the richness of Rick Moss' work. The quotes are magnificent, but then he acts so compassionately to share meditations and examples of clearings that are perfect. This will change people's lives. The format is also well done. Each chapter begins sweetly, and becomes deeper in a natural way until the reader is receptive to a big shift in consciousness. Many thanks for all the effort."

~ **Bill Little, PhD**, Spiritual Director, Center for Spiritual Awakening and Speaker

"In addition to giving us clear, accessible information about the Roots of Wisdom, Dr. Moss has skillfully and thoughtfully opened many doors that will enable us to discover more of our own wisdom as well as that of the 'masters'. I have been waiting for a self-help book that thinks this well about the reader's process and journey. This is a book of beautiful, helpful and inspiring bridges to awakening. "

~ **Fred Jealous**, Founder and Teacher, Breakthrough Men's Community

DROPS
OF
WISDOM

Guidance On the Path Of Awakening

Rick Moss, PhD

"In *Drops of Wisdom,* a spiritual manual distilled from a lifetime of practice, Rick Moss combines directness and evocativeness into a powerful collaged statement that invites participation. The teachings of the masters whom he presents serve as catalysts for experiencing, relating and connecting to God. Each quotation is like a grain of sand in Blake's *Auguries of Innocence*: he sees a world in it as he 'holds infinity in the palm of [his] hand' and extends that hand to his reader. His descriptions of the Clearing practice that he initiated attest to his own mastery and inspire trust in what he has to offer: a path of spiritual transformation leading to the true self."

~ **Marc Kaminsky**, psychotherapist, poet, and author of *A Cleft in the Rock*

"While reading *Drops of Wisdom*, I notice that Rick Moss's writing has a depth of meaning that resonates in my body. I literally feel the truth of his words in my bones. I can't help but think, 'I want more Drops of Wisdom!'"

~ **Tom North**, Author, financial consultant, and a leader of Break through Men's work.

"*Drops of Wisdom* is like a precious gem in its rarity and brilliance. Rick Moss writes with crisp clarity on qualities that we all yearn for in our personal relationships with ourselves and others.

Rick shines a light toward a way that we can truly live in peace, love and happiness.

This book is for anyone who is interested in deepening their connection to their divine nature and expanding their consciousness from the limitations of the ego."

~**Josephine Littlefield**, LCSW, psychotherapist.

For all who are seeking the wisdom and experience of their own Divine Nature.

DROPS
OF
WISDOM

TABLE OF CONTENTS

Introduction

Drops of Wisdom exist in the moments when the Divine speaks through us. Our human egos can repeat, embroider, and even expand upon ideas they contain. But, that spark of Insight, Beauty, Truth and Grace is not born of the ego, but of Divine consciousness.

It's these drops of insight and wisdom that I have been drawn to ever since Paramahansa Yogananda's "Autobiography of a Yogi" awoke something deep inside me and I began meditating in the 1970s.

The first seeds for this book were sown while I was writing my PhD dissertation on "Education and the Growth of Consciousness" at the University of Texas. As I read through books and articles on Consciousness, I discovered many brilliant quotes and ideas, and I began to keep file boxes of these quotes, which seemed like jewel boxes to me.

Upon completing my PhD, I continued copying those brilliant quotes on three-by-five cards, filed them alphabetically by topic, and eventually shared those "drops of wisdom" with my clients in my counseling practice.

After about 20 years of full-time involvement in meditation, I experienced a life-changing realization. I taught and believed that all one had to do was to transcend, experience Pure Consciousness, and all of one's life would improve and be transformed. I had taught this fervently; but, I could not deny that this wasn't true for me.

I craved for emotional connections that weren't there, despite being married to a wonderful person, I felt that my emotional development was limited. Generally, I was a caring person, but my ability to provide unconditional love was plainly restricted. Of extreme concern to me was the fact that in addition to many physical ailments and food allergies, I had no personal relationship with God.

I developed the ability to perform self-muscle testing during this time. When I asked myself a question, my neck would move up and down to indicate yes and sideways to indicate no. I primarily used this ability to determine which foods I could digest and which vitamins my body required at the time.

Because of my personal issues, I sought out new teachers, and discovered how muscle testing could reveal our hidden beliefs.

I realized that we have the ability to change our thoughts, limiting beliefs and the patterns they create in our lives. My neck muscle testing ability proved to be very accurate. I didn't just get yes or no answers; I also felt like I was receiving Divine Guidance.

When I first started sharing these ideas with others, they regularly told me how beneficial it was in helping them change and heal. Without realizing it, I began a new career and a new life, calling my work Pre-Cognitive Re-Education. Pre-Cognitive because it emphasized the unconscious, and Re-Education because the goal was to re-train and encourage people to go within to find solutions to life's challenges.

For over 35 years, I have continued this work, and have led over 15,000 personal sessions. I now refer to the work I do as Awakening Greatness.

My experiences working with clients has provided me with many insights and experiences that I happily share in the pages ahead. The quotes I collected were often exactly what my clients needed to hear in order to make a change or adjust their perspectives.

I was frequently directed as to which quote to use. I began to collect them in a small book, and this small book has grown into the one you are now reading.

My family and I left our TM group by 1990 and moved to California. It was at that time that I began to investigate new worlds of healing, growth and transformation. I learned from, and am deeply grateful to many spiritual teachers since my life-changing time with Maharishi Mahesh Yogi.

You will find their names and quotes throughout this book. Among them are Shri Shri Ravi Shankar, Mata Amritanandamayi (Ammaji), Devaji, Panache Desai, Carl Jung, Ramakrishna and Menachem Mendel Schneerson.

Turning Knowledge Into Wisdom

I suggest that those of you who wish to immerse yourselves in the timeless wisdom of the many jewel-like quotes contained in this book should take your time digesting them.

Don't speed through them or read them hastily. Let them seep through you. Perhaps read them aloud to yourself or to someone else. These quotations serve as a repository for the world's most profound wisdom. Enjoy them. Such focus will assist you in translating the author's advice into your own wisdom.

To give structure and purpose to the quotes, I have created a framework based on my experiences, growth, and work with the clients I have served. I hope that each chapter is the beginning of a discussion and not the end. I also have provided questions to encourage you to examine your beliefs before you explore the quotes.

Take part in each chapter's activities if you wish to benefit personally and spiritually from this book. The exercises assist in opening a healing door to your unconscious mind, in addition to providing an opportunity for transformation in the conscious mind. They will help you to better know your ego and Self more deeply

Each chapter has a section called "An Integration". My heart reveals its poetry here, and the wisdom that flows through me is given its freest expression. Hopefully, this section resonates with you on a deeper level. The final section of each chapter ends with "In Essence". This summary is intended to help you review key concepts for further thought and contemplation.

Regarding the Language in This Book

For clarity's sake, I use the word unconscious for that which we are not conscious of. I reserve the word subconscious for the part of the unconscious more accessible to the conscious mind.

For words like Love, Peace, Spirit, and Truth, I use a capital letter. This capitalization denotes something that has a Divine source as opposed to the egoic version of the attribute.

Throughout the book, I've used words like "Divine", "Source", "Creator" and "Void" for those who may struggle with the word "God". You may substitute whatever word you prefer.

Many of my clients have found it beneficial if I explain my understanding of the word God. First and foremost, I realize that anything I say about the nature of God is limited, and therefore, imperfect.

My understanding of the Divine is that it is infinite, omnipresent and manifests as everything. Therefore, any words I may use to describe the indescribable, are merely a finger pointing towards the moon and not the moon itself.

With that being said, let me say that I believe God is our creator and source of all goodness. I do not believe that God is judging us, just as I believe that Love, an emanation of God, has no capacity to judge.

A Brief Overview
of Each Chapter

There are several over-lighting Truths that form a central core of this book, particularly Chapters One, Three, Four and Ten.

It's important to understand the distinction between ego-based love (spelled with a lower-case "l") and Love of a Divine origin (spelled with a capital "L").

If you remember one thing from this book, it's the importance of Great-Love to enrich, bless and transform your life for the rest of your life.

The first chapter, *Great-Love*, seeks to distinguish unconditional Great-Love from the ego's version of love. We will explore the importance of understanding the distinction between love and Great-Love, and why we often resist Great-Love.

Chapter Two is an invitation to explore and possibly answer the most important spiritual question: *Who am I?* We will expand our sense of what Self may be to help us go beyond the ego.

In Chapter Three, we go deeply into the issue of *Healing the Hurt Child Within*. In over 30 years of practice, it is abundantly clear to me that personal and spiritual growth is restricted, and perhaps unachievable when the hurts and wounds of childhood capture the ego-mind.

Chapter Four is about the power of *Forgiveness* and how forgiveness frees our Soul as it supports us and others in remembering who we and they really are

The fifth Chapter, *The Creator Perspective,* looks at the idea and benefits of seeing ourselves as creators of our life experiences instead of the egoic perspective of being a victim..

Chapter Six is about *God*. It attempts to help us connect to the Divine more deeply while examining our conscious and unconscious resistance to God.

Chapter Seven explores different kinds of *Prayer*. An emphasis is placed on prayer as a means for conscious connection to the Divine, to the Void and to the Absolute.

In Chapter Eight, we will dive into the two stages of *Spiritual Growth* - what supports it and what limits it.

Chapter Nine focuses on *Enlightenment*. It is an attempt to clarify what enlightenment is, and what the differing states of enlightenment may be.

In Chapter 10, I invite you to explore how to make *Relationships* thrive, their value to maturity, and the growth of consciousness. The chapter offers four approaches to help relationships thrive.

Chapter 11 tackles *Healing* the Mind/Body and Soul. It includes an opportunity to examine if you are resisting your healing.

Chapter 12 discusses the power of *Gratitude*. It is an astonishing tool recognized by brain science and spirituality to transform your life experience.

Chapter 13 invites you to explore *Genuine Happiness* - happiness that comes from within, happiness that doesn't fade or lead to addiction.

In Chapter 14, we take a loving and gentle step into *Stillness*. In Stillness, we will find Peace that passes understanding. And yet, how we resist and fear the quiet and run from the Stillness.

And finally, in Chapter 15, we come to *Grace*. Could it be that All is given to us, but we resist such a gift? However, we will undoubtedly only know only that blessing of Grace that we can receive.

In each chapter, you will find exercises and processes to support you in making the information personally relevant and useful.

More than any other part of a chapter, the Integration feels to me like a blessing from beyond my personal mind.

Although I wrote this book for me, my hope with this book is that it finds its way into receptive minds and appreciative hearts. Working with these Drops of Wisdom has been deeply rewarding and exquisitely pleasurable. I imagine it might be parallel to a jeweler savoring handfuls of precious gems.

I hope you find many treasures here.

Chapter 1

GREAT-LOVE

The Difference Between Great-Love and Egoic-love

G reat-Love heals. Great-Love transforms. It is God in action. Into dark spaces, Great-Love brings Light. Into shame and judgment, it brings forgiveness. Great-Love is a mother's unconditional embrace and a father's unreserved steadfastness.

Great-Love is felt when our dog greets us upon our return, and is felt when our cat comes to sit on our lap when we are crying. Great-Love can be experienced through deep friendships, selfless service, intimate relationships and through immersion in Nature.

When brought to painful childhood memories lodged in the unconscious, Great-Love is the energy that clears, frees, and rights them. It releases the past and opens the door to the present. It judges nothing. It includes everything.

Self-Inquiry Questions:

- Have you ever Loved someone or something so much that your focus was entirely on them?

- Have you ever, perhaps just for a moment, melted in Love and lost your sense of separation?

- Have you ever felt completely accepted, just as you are?

- How would the people in your life change if they felt Loved by you?

Quotes About This Extraordinary Experience Called Great-Love

"The moment you have in your heart this extraordinary thing called love and feel the depth, the delight, the ecstasy of it, you will discover that for you the world is transformed"

~ Jiddu Krishnamurti

"Through the power of love, we can let go of past history and begin again. Love heals, forgives, and makes whole."

~ Ernest Holmes

"The supreme purpose and goal for human life is to cultivate love."

~Ramakrishna

"Of all powers, love is the most powerful and the most powerless. It is the most powerful because it alone can conquer that final and most impregnable stronghold which is the human heart. It is the most powerless because it can do nothing except by consent."

~Frederick Buechner

"Our survival depends on the healing power of love, intimacy and relationships. As individuals. As communities. As a country. As a culture. Perhaps even as a species."

~Dean Ornish

"Love is life. All, everything that I understand, I understand only because I love. Everything is, everything exists, only because I love. Everything is united by it alone. Love is God, and to die means that I, a particle of love, shall return to the general and eternal source."

~Leo Tolstoy

"Don't forget love; it will bring all the madness you need, to unfurl yourself across the universe."

~Mirabai

The Difference Between Egoic-love and Great-Love

Our ego knows nothing about Great-Love. Its version of love (with a lowercase 'l') is focused on getting what it wants. Our ego's version of love is transactional; it keeps score: I give this, you provide that. Ego-based love is about what our ego gets from something. The more it gets what it wants, the more it loves what it receives.

Great-Love flows with no demands or conditions. The giver is fulfilled in the giving alone without needing anything back. Its source is Divine. Some may call that source God, others Buddha or Nature, while some may call it the Absolute or Pure Being.

Understanding the distinction between love and Great-Love is fundamental. Removing the blocks to Great-Love is essential. It will be the greatest achievement of this or any lifetime. It is this Great-Love that heals, transforms and fulfills. We know God through this Great-Love.

Allow me to reaffirm that there is nothing wrong with egoic-love. Romantic, head-over-heels love might be the most exciting experience that our egos have. Generally, in the head-over-heels experience, the ego is thinking, *'finally, with this person, I'm going to get what I've dreamed of forever.'* Sadly (or happily from the growth perspective), it doesn't feel like that for long.

Many relationships fall apart when the ego-romance begins to wane, and the work of personal maturity needed for Great-Love begins. Romantic-love, however, can become an integral part of a committed relationship, as we will explore in the chapter on Relationships.

In our English-speaking world, it is common to use the word "love" for many separate and very distinct things. The ego uses the word love to mean something that gives it pleasure, excitement, or some other form of gratification.

For example, my ego might think, *'I love chocolate ice cream.'* What my ego means is that I love what I get, what I experience from eating chocolate ice cream.

My ego might say to my partner, "I love you." What my ego means by saying, "I love you," is based on what I get from our relationship. That may include a sense of safety, excitement, and completion, etc. Again, my ego is always interested in, 'what am I getting?'

Perhaps a more accurate word for egoic-love, so as not to confuse it with Great-Love, is the word "like." *'I really like chocolate ice cream,'* clearly acknowledges that I am, through the experience of eating, getting something from which I take lots of pleasure. And, this is wonderful. However, it is a very different experience from Great-Love.

No one outside of ourselves can provide us with everything we need and want. It might feel like that at the beginning of an exciting, new relationship. Yet, after a while, we may think we are falling out of love because our egoic misperceptions start to re-emerge. Lasting, successful, fulfilling human relationships are a combination of egoic-love, personal preferences and Great-Love that asks for nothing and offers unquestioning support, care, kindness, honesty and presence.

To further clarify, our egos do not manufacture Great-Love. In fact, it is not created by us at all. Great-Love is God's power in action through us; it is our True Nature. It is the natural response of the Self to Life. In Loving-Unconditionally, we just permit this Great-Love to pass through us to others.

Great-Love is the opposite of egoic-love. It is all about giving. Great-Love is given to another without demands or expectations. There are no conditions attached to it. When we genuinely give Great-Love, we want nothing in return. However, much like all spiritual experiences, we do get back precisely what we freely give. In short, we experience Great-Love by unreservedly giving it away to others. We also share in Great-Love by allowing others to Love us Unconditionally.

Perhaps, the Buddha described the difference between like, or egoic-love and Great-Love when he said, "If we like a flower, we pick it. If we love a flower, we water it."

We may experience Great-Love when we focus on a person, an animal, a tree, or even something in Nature. When our egos shrink, our awareness expands, and so does our awareness of Great-Love. It grows to include more and more of everything. Great-Love is all-inclusive.

As Rumi wrote, "There are no edges to my loving now".

Perhaps the greatest challenge to Great-Love that we face is with our children. Our egos have strong needs for them to be and act in a certain way. I believe we perceive them as reflections of ourselves, and egoically, we wish they, and us, would be seen in a positive light. Our children's failures and challenges have such a strong impact on us, that we wish to control them for theirs and our sake.

This and other egoic needs obscure our innate capacity to Love Unconditionally. With egoic love, we value and appreciate more under certain circumstances, and we appreciate and value less under others.

I have an acquaintance who is a perfect example of ego-love versus Great-Love. For the sake of anonymity, we'll say that he is a lawyer. He values clear thinking, competition, high status and large income. He has a son. His son is artistic, feeling-oriented, and not interested in being a lawyer. However, his father wants the boy to be a reflection of him and enjoy life the way he does. The father tells his son he will only pay for college if he agrees to put away his fantasies and become a lawyer. My acquaintance believes he is loving his son and fulfilling his fatherly duty.

Great-Love embraces and accepts what it beholds. If the father was experiencing Great-Love he could fully appreciate and nurture qualities in his son that are different from his own qualities. He also could share his vision of what is important to him; but, manipulation would *never* be an outcome of Great-Love.

Exploring Resistance to Great-Love

Why then, would our egos build barriers to Great-Love? Some of us believe that we do not deserve to be loved in this unconditional way. Often, we were taught as children, usually by parents, that we only get love when we perform or act in a certain manner. In this way, we may unconsciously equate love with having to behave inauthentically.

Additionally, if we have been hurt by the people who were supposed to love and care for us, even now, we will protect our hearts from love, as we imagine it to be based on the past.

Many of us have been taught that it is egotistical and shameful to love ourselves. However, if we cannot love ourselves, then we cannot love others, or let others love us. All of the examples previously mentioned reveal that we protect ourselves from what we perceive love to be based on what we experienced as children.

Quotes About, Unconditional and Great-Love

"Your task is not to seek for love, but merely to seek and find all the barriers within yourself that you have built against it."

~Rumi

"I love you, and it's no concern of yours."

~Maharishi Mahesh Yogi

"The only thing I know that truly heals people is unconditional love."

~Elisabeth Kübler-Ross

"True love does not run. True love does not move. It receives absolutely everything exactly the same."

~Devaji

"Divine love is not polluted by desires. Personal love is mixed with attachment."

~Baba Hari Dass"

"If in a relationship you experience both 'love' and the opposite of love – attack, emotional violence, and so on – then it is likely that you are confusing ego attachment and addictive clinging with love."

~Eckhart Tolle

"True love has no opposite. If your 'love' has an opposite, then it is not love but a strong ego-need for a more complete and deeper sense of self, a need that the other person temporarily meets. It is the ego's substitute for salvation, and for a short time it almost does feel like salvation."

~Eckhart Tolle

Love in fact is the spiritual life, and without it all the other exercises of the spirit, however lofty, are emptied of content and become mere illusions."

~Thomas Merton

"Someday, after mastering the winds, the waves, the tides and gravity, we shall harness for God the energies of love, and then, for a second time in the history of the world, man will have discovered fire."

~Pierre Teilhard De Chardin

"In true love there is no heartbreak. A broken heart means broken demands, broken expectations and broken hopes."

~Sri Sri Ravi Shankar

"There is love and Love. You love your family — your father, mother, sister, brother, husband, wife, etc. But you do not love your neighbor. You love your son or daughter, but you do not love all children. You love your father and mother, but you do not love everyone the way you love your father and mother. You love your religion, but you do not love all religions. Likewise, you have love for your country, but you do not love all countries. Hence, this is not Love; it is only love. Transformation of this love to Love is the goal of spirituality. In the fullness of Love blossoms the beautiful, fragrant flower of compassion."

~Mātā Amritānandamayī (Amma) Devī

"So I see it's true: all objects in existence are wildly in love."

~Meister Eckhart

Exploring Great-Love More Deeply With the Work Of Author David Richo

Let's explore Great-Love in a very straightforward and practical approach, as created by psychotherapist and author David Richo.

Dr. Richo shares a clarifying insight in his excellent book, *How to Be an Adult in Relationships - Five Keys to Mindful Loving.*

He suggests there are basically five essential elements of Great-Love. He calls them the **Five A's. of Love.** They are :

1. Attention

2. Acceptance

3. Appreciation

4. Affection

5. Allowing

Unconditional Love is given when these Five A's are given.

Let's look a little more deeply at each of the Five A's as it pertains to Great-Love.

1. Giving **Attention** is a mindful and conscious state, and helps with the practice of being in the moment. The highest value of given Attention is called Free-Attention. In Free-Attention, the giver has no agenda for the receiver. The giver's mind is in the present time, and the intent is just to be with the receiver without expectations. It offers the giver an experience of selflessness.

Receiving Genuine Attention may enhance one's sense of self-respect and a feeling of safety. It allows the receiver to explore his or her Attention needs and desires.

2. Giving **Acceptance** requires that the giver is capable of choosing to be in a state of non-judgment. It offers the giver an experience of openness and compassion that is beyond the ego's capacity. In this unconditionality, it can be a spiritually connective experience.

Receiving Acceptance is something that many people have never fully experienced. If, in our childhood, we had judgmental, critical or absent parents, we likely emerged with a conscious or unconscious feeling that we are not enough. We may not allow ourselves to receive Acceptance if we feel we are not okay.

To compensate for this lack, we may attempt to "earn" the Acceptance of others. But, anything–we have to earn, can just as easily be taken away. Unconditional Great-Love and Acceptance are never based on performance or earning.

Giving and Receiving Full Acceptance looks beyond the personality, and accepts the Divine Being exactly as it is, entirely. Receiving and giving Acceptance nurtures our feelings of self-worth.

3. Giving **Appreciation** at the highest level is not about what our ego or head might value, like someone who dresses in clothes we find attractive, or has attractive bodily features; although there is certainly nothing wrong with this level of Appreciation.

At the highest level, without ego, Appreciation is more about what moves our hearts to say, "I so appreciate your kindness and generosity, your trustworthiness, and your ability to give to those in need." These qualities are the deep and unchanging aspects of our Best Selves. What we see in another, we are able to strengthen in ourselves.

Receiving Appreciation encourages us to recognize and connect with qualities that we may not have noticed or acknowledged within ourselves. It enlivens self-worth. Also, Appreciation can give us a feeling of a warm glow. It can feel like an acknowledgment of our goodness. It can help us feel safe.

4. Giving **Affection** enriches our hearts and fills us with the sweetness we are giving. In filling us with this sweetness, we can feel that every part of our body is being nurtured and bathed in goodness.

Receiving Affection is the warm honey of Great-Love. It can take us back to the loving arms of a mother, father or caring person. It can also begin to replace any lack of Affection that may have been experienced in early life. The replacement effect of Affection can only work if it is within the presence of the other four A's, for then it feels safe to let Great-Love into such deep levels of our Being.

5.   Giving **Allowing** frees the giver from having to fix anything. It says, "I accept who you are and where you are in your journey."

An example of Allowing might be a parent who loves being a doctor and dreams of their child following in their footsteps, but gives up their preferences to allow their offspring to follow their own path.

Receiving Allowing frees the receiver of having to please and compromise their own feelings and needs without the risk of being rejected. It helps us to feel free.

Great-Love, Unconditional Love contains all five A's. If one or more of the five A's are missing, Great-Love becomes warped and reduced to nothing more than a strategy for getting what the ego believes it wants, or must have to be happy.

Writer and teacher Marc Gafni pointed out that, "When we mistake a part for the whole, we pathologize the part."

For example, a common misperception is that Appreciation and Affection feel like Great-Love. They certainly feel good to the ego, but they are not Great-Love.

If someone only feels "loved" when they are continually receiving or giving Appreciation and Affection, then they are in a highly needy state. And, most likely, they are experiencing a profound lack of self-worth, possibly generated from an unresolved lack of positive and loving childhood experiences.

In a case like that, a person may feel loved, but only for a moment. Because, momentary compensation for the absence of Great-Love is shallow and fleeting. In some ways, it is parallel to a drug-induced high. Within a short time, the effects wear off as if nothing was given or received at all.

If we mistake one of the five A's, like Appreciation or Affection, for the totality of Great-Love, or all of the five A's together, then we pathologize

Appreciation or Affection, or any of the five A's to which we have grown over-attached.

Just as we need the five food groups to be physically, mentally and emotionally healthy, we also need the five A's for much the same reasons. If we make dessert, or just one or two of the five A's, the totality of our meals, we will become ill.

Self-Inquiry Questions:

- What are some of the consequences I felt when Great-Love was not experienced, especially in my childhood?
- How do I feel when I perceive that I am not Loved?
- How would the people in my life change if they felt Loved by me?
- What am I willing to do to live in a constant state of Great-Love?

Quotes About the Need for Great-Love

"For the most part, mental illness is caused by an absence of or a defect in the love that a particular child required from its particular parents for successful maturation and spiritual growth. It."

~M. Scott Peck, MD

"If one remains on a journey of spiritual growth, one's capacity to love grows and grows. One clearly should not attempt psychotherapy beyond one's capacity to love, since psychotherapy without love will be unsuccessful and even harmful."

~M. Scott Peck, MD

"What is hell? I maintain that it is the suffering of being unable to love."

~Fyodor Dostoyevsky

"It's not the perfect but the imperfect that is in need of our love."

~Oscar Wilde

"It is impossible to enter a state of peace without love. Love is the only reality there is."

~Ernest Holmes

"Teach us to care, and not to care."

~T.S. Eliot

"Whatever you're doing to be loved is what is keeping you from being loved. There is no authentic life without authentic Love."

~Rick Moss

"It is only with the heart that one can see rightly; what is essential is invisible to the eye."

~Antoine de Saint-Exupéry

"When I see that I am nothing, that is wisdom. When I see that I am everything, that is love. And between these two, my life flows."

~Nisargadatta Maharaj

"The unconditional presence of someone who loves us harkens back to the past and repairs our childhood sense of being unwanted."

~David Richo

"Hatred never ceases by hatred; by love alone is it healed."

~Buddhist saying

"Whoever does not love does not know God, because God is love.

~John 4:8 (*From The New International version of The Bible*)

"When we come to the last moment of this lifetime, and we look back across it, the only thing that's going to matter is 'What is the quality of our love'"?

~Richard Bach

"Add LOVE… Then wilt thou not be loth

To leave this Paradise, but shall possess

A Paradise within thee, happier far."

~John Milton

"When you love with the heart of God, you think with the mind of God."

~Rick Moss

An Experiential Opportunity for Great-Love: An Inner Child Healing

Recall a time, if you will, a time when you were feeling unappreciated, unloved, hurt by others' expectations, left out, or afraid.

1. Explore that feeling as if it is a moment from your personal childhood experience. We can call this encapsulated moment an Inner Child Moment.

2. Explore the feelings, but stay separate from the child you envision.

Now, imagine this child is about six or seven years old. They are sitting on their bed, and they are alone. The child is feeling one, or more, or all of the emotions mentioned above.

1. Visualize the posture of this child, feeling the emotions you recalled from your childhood.

2. Observe the child from the part of you that is the most caring, most kind and most trustworthy.

To quickly find this compassionate part within, ask yourself, "When do I most feel this way"? It might be with your own child, with your pet, in Nature, or with a friend.

1. Be aware of the feeling of caring or kindness or Great-Love within you and direct it to the hurting child on the bed whose posture you imagined.

Now, as your best compassionate self, reach out to the child and say: "Of course you are feeling what you're feeling. You have every right to feel the way you do. You have not always had someone on your side, who without fail, has your best interests in mind and heart. That's why I have come; I'm the one Great-Love has sent to love you always."

1. Observe what the child's posture is now.

2. Continue communicating with the child, "Everyone is meant to have at least one person to love them 24/7, and I am yours. I am sorry that it couldn't be your mother or father, but they just didn't have the ability to show you Unconditional Love 24/7. "

No parent can, when they are raising children and working, and there are a million demands upon daily life. But I am capable because I am the grown-up you, and I love you unconditionally and I am your 24/7 person.

Spend a little imagined time with this child and answer these questions.

1. Would they like to be held by you?

2. Have they started to trust you yet?

3. Are they open to having your arm around them?

4. Would they like to play with you, or go for a walk?

Examine what you are feeling for this child.

1. Does it feel like it has an end?

2. Does it feel safe?

3. Does it feel like Unconditional Love?

4. Could you imagine feeling this way about this child and intentionally harming this child?

5. Does it feel good to you to give this child Unconditional Love?

6. Are your feelings protective and nurturing?

If you answered yes, then it is Great-Love, expressed through your Best Self.

When offered in a repeatable manner, it will heal that Inner Child Moment, which will evolve to be part of your awakened heart.See Chapter Three for more about Healing the Wounded Child.

An Integration

Our egos are very confused about what Great-Love truly is. This is for a very simple reason; our egos are not capable of Unconditional Love.

Our egos can certainly 'like' very intently, even to the point where it may feel to us like Love. But everything our egos want and like is self-serving; it is precisely for what it gives to our egos.

Egoic liking is ultimately about what the ego gets in life - what feelings of pleasure, self-gratification and other such egoic benefits. It can be confusing, because our like and Love experiences can get mixed together and experienced simultaneously. One thing's for certain - Great-Love is not known, cannot be known by the ego. We know when we are just experiencing Great, Unconditional Love. We feel expanded, free and blissful.

Great-Love is the natural state of our True-Selves. Our True-Self is an individual expression of the Source of Love, of God, of Goddess and of the Divine.

When we have an oceanic experience of Great-Love emanating from our True-Selves, it is clear that it transcends a combination of like and Love. It is Love without a 'but', without a condition, without limitation. It is all 'give'.

God is All Give all of the time. God loves as the sun shines; the sun asks for nothing in return. The sun judges not what it shines upon. It is the basis of life, and as such, everything that lives has the sun within it. Just as everything that exists has God within it. Everything has its Self in God.

Great-Love appears in many flavors, many forms and many expressions. However, all of these flavors, forms, and expressions have one unquestionable thing in common: Great-Love cannot harm. Anything generated from Great-Love is all Good regardless of how it might appear or feel to our limited egoic perceptions.

Love is Good. And Good is God. God is Love. All. The. Time.

In Essence

At the most fundamental level, there is love and Great-Love. Great-Love is impersonal.

It embraces and accepts everything it observes in another.

Its Source transcends humanness.

A spiritual person might call this source God or Buddha-nature.

On the other hand, personal or egoic-love is a response to a person or thing for qualities that benefit us or give us pleasure.

This is egocentric love.

Those who have known both kinds - Love and love, assure us that Love is the Source, the course, and the goal of human experience.

Chapter 2

WHO AM I?

―

We set out in life trying to discover who we are. What are our gifts? What makes us unique and special? When we're successful in developing and expressing our egoic identity, we grow stronger in our sense of a personal self (which we'll refer to with a small "s").

Over time, however, this sense of self can feel limiting and unfulfilling. It can feel like a shoe that we have outgrown. For many of us, we begin to hear a spiritual calling from within to discover a higher, innate and transcendental Self.

People, teachers and books begin to show up. We have come to a spiritual fork in the road. If we take this path, our lives will never be quite the same. It may feel like we're going Home. It might feel like we're touching our Soul.

As we delve into this chapter, we will engage in an Experiential Opportunity to see if we can enrich and expand our sense of what this Self might be.

Self-Inquiry Questions

- Am I willing to explore a Self beyond what I believe is myself?
- What might I be afraid to lose?
- Am I willing to awaken if that means I will be different from others?
- Can I begin to imagine total Freedom and complete Peace?

Quotes About Self-Discovery: The Great Journey Begins

"There's something safe about playing a character, but then it's like, 'Who am I underneath?'"

~Emmy Rossum

"The true nature of our soul is obscured by three things: Desire, intellect, and ego. These three things obscure the [higher] self, and meditation is where you just freeze these three things for a few moments."

~Shri Shri Ravi Shankar

"Before you figure out who you are, you have to figure out who you aren't."

~Iyanla Vanzant

"The fish in water that is thirsty needs serious professional counseling."

~Kabir *(Translated by Daniel Ladinsky)*

"The truth is that we are not one person, but many people in one. In fact, the most accurate way to think of ourselves is that we exist as a broad set of potentialities, rather than as a narrow set of traits…This means that it may not be possible to know ourselves to any meaningful level of specificity…"

~Raj Raghunathan

The ego and the non-conscious may well be unknowable in any factual way. There may be too much hidden from conscious awareness. But, this does not mean that the egoic fragmentation needs to keep us from knowing our True Self.

"Each of us constructs and lives a 'narrative.' This narrative is us, our identities."

~Oliver Sacks

The 'narrative,' which Oliver Sacks refers to above, is our limited self-constructed identity. It is who the ego thinks we are based on our unexamined, retained-past, both conscious and non-conscious. Many people stop their questioning of who they are with a sense of their identity just based on the past. In growing, they can explore beyond the ego to their innate and unchangeable True Identity.

"I recognize that I am made up of several persons and that the person that at the moment has the upper hand will inevitably give place to another. But which is the real one? All of them or none?"

~W. Somerset Maugham

"I am larger, better than I thought, I did not know I held so much goodness."

~Walt Whitman

Who Am I?

As our journey unfolds, we naturally begin to ask ourselves questions, such as:

- Who am I?

- Who am I beyond my ego?

- What is, or lives beyond my ego?

- What part of me is the Divinely-given qualities that make up my Greatness?

Even though the personal self - the ego - may seem like a cosmic illusion, it is essential in a key part of our journey towards awakening. We cannot let go of the ego, and live as the Self while the ego is still fragmented and immature.

At a public lecture, I heard Maharishi Mahesh Yogi describe the ego as being like a boat that gets one across the river. You wouldn't want to give up the boat halfway. It's critical to your survival. Yet, when you get across the river safely, you just naturally let go of your attachment to the boat.

Our ego serves an essential survival role in our growing maturity and evolution. Once it has served its purpose, it is time to let go of our limited sense of ourselves in favor of discovering a sense of our identity in our Higher-Self, which we could also call our Soul.

The ego still remains after enlightenment, even though our identity shifts to our Higher-Self. We still have preferences. An ego, however faint, helps us to stay on the planet.

It may sound strange, even frightening, to think that we are not this ego we have come to know and call home. There was a time when I might have agreed with you.

One afternoon during a workshop, we were asked to pick a partner and just stare into their eyes. After about five minutes, something started happening. I started to lose my sense of the room. My next thought was, where do I know this person from? It's not here and now. Suddenly, I felt this sense of spaciousness, and I didn't feel like I was looking into someone's eyes anymore.

There just was a sense of wholeness, and I was a part of that wholeness; and for a few moments, there was no I, just the wholeness. It wasn't frightening. It was wonderful. And then, there I was again. It was very short, but it was profoundly reassuring. I didn't need an ego to be.

Quotes About Self-Discovery: The Higher Version of Self

"I am larger, better than I thought, I did not know I held so much goodness."

~Walt Whitman

"You were born with potential. You were born with goodness and trust. You were born with Greatness. You were born with wings. You are not meant for crawling, so don't. You have wings. Learn to use them and fly."

~Rumi

"Doing what needs to be done may not make you happy, but it will make you great."

~George Bernard Shaw

"Integral education is based on the understanding that at our inmost center there is a free being, wide and knowing, who awaits our discovery and who ought to become the acting center of our being and our life."

~Sri Aurobindo

"Sometimes, it takes great suffering to pierce the soul and open it up to greatness."

~Jocelyn Murray

"… we cannot achieve greatness unless we lose all interest in being great. For our own idea of Greatness is illusory…"

~Thomas Merton

"Relationship to the Self is at once a relationship to our fellow man, and no one can be related to the latter until he is related to himself."

~Carl Jung

"There is no paycheck that can equal the feeling of contentment that comes from being the person you are meant to be."

~Oprah Winfrey

"It's only when you hitch your wagon to something larger than yourself that you realize your true potential."

~Barack Obama

"When the brain's potential is fully unleashed, there can be few if any limitations."

~James Morcan

"If you have will-power, then you can do anything. It is usually said that you are your own master."

~H.H. The Dalai Lama

"Every human has four endowments – self-awareness, conscience, independent will and creative imagination. These give us the ultimate human freedom…the power to choose, to respond, to change."

~Stephen Covey

"Never underestimate the power of dreams, and the influence of the human spirit. We are all the same in this notion: The potential for greatness lives within each of us."

~Wilma Rudolph

"Humanity has only scratched the surface of its real potential."

~Peace Pilgrim

"The past is not your potential. In any hour you can choose to liberate the future."

~Marilyn Ferguson

"And what is the potential [hu]man, after all? Is he not the sum of all that is human? Divine, in other words."

~Henry Miller

Our Work

It can be difficult for our immature egos to accept the possibility of inner Greatness because our egos have nothing to do with it. In fact, they are the obstacles to its realization and expression. Fear, jealousy, lust, addiction, blame, resentment, and a whole host of other ego states fixate our awareness in the remembered past, and therefore, in the limited mind.

Our work is to free the damaged ego from its contracted state so that our inherent nature, which has within it all of God's gifts to us, can flow freely into the world. In my experience, this growth and freedom are deeply supported by the continued experience of our True Self.

A Meditative Process: Who Am I?

Start by quieting your mind and body.

1. On an in-breath, breathe in stillness.

2. On an out-breath, breathe out tension. Do this until you feel yourself relaxing.

Pose the question to yourself, 'Who am I?'

1. With every answer you get, just notice it and let it go and ask again, 'Who am I?'

2. Change the inflection of the question by emphasizing the word "Who" and then on the word, "Am" and on the word, "I."

After you start to run out of answers…then ask: Who am I, *Really*? If there is no clear answer, just be with the absence of an answer.

Two Masters Offer Guidance

"The question 'Who am I' has no answer. No experience can answer it, for the self is beyond experience. It has no answer in consciousness and, therefore, helps (us) to go beyond consciousness."

~Sri Nisargadatta Maharaj

"Just feel your Self. Where are you really? Can you find someone? From where is the looking arising? Then all that remains is the beauty of receiving the Beloved everywhere."

~Devaji

Who Am I Truly?

Beyond Egoic-Identity to the One-Self

"The truth is you really are nothing, but this nothing is full, whole, infinite in everything and everywhere."

~Gangaji

"The seemingly solid, concrete, independent, self-instituting I under its own power that appears, actually does not exist at all."

~H.H. Dalai Lama

"I promise you, there is no personal self."

~Devaji

"I have no seams, no walls, no laws. My frontiers and God's are the same."

~Saint Teresa de Jesus of Avila

"The deepest you is the nothing inside, the side which you don't know. Don't be afraid of nothing."

~Alan Watts

"You have no choice. You must leave your ego on the doorstep before you enter love."

~Kamand Kojouri

My me is God, nor do I recognize any other Me except my God Himself,

~Saint Catherine of Genoa

"The mystic knows that the essence of prayer is the hidden secret, "I am He whom I love, He whom I love is me."

~Llewellyn Vaughan-Lee

"There is no such thing as a person. There are only restrictions and limitations. The sum total of these defines the person. You think you know yourself when you know what you are. But you never know who you are. The person merely appears to be, like the space within the pot appears to have the shape and volume and smell of the pot".

~Sri Nisargadatta Maharaj

"You are the entire universe. You are in all, and all is in you. Sun, moon, and stars are revolving in you."

~Swami Muktananda

"The world is a mountain, in which your words are echoed back to you."

~Rumi

"Every person is a microcosm of the entire Creation."

~Rebbe Menachem Mendel Schneerson

"The truth of who we are lies far beyond even the greatest dharmas, the greatest sutras, the greatest ideas that could ever be spoken or written down or read."

~Adyashanti

"In a breakthrough, I find that God and I are both the same…"

~Meister Eckhart

"I most certainly believe that it is the gift of God that I am what I am."

~Saint Patrick

"What a liberation to realize that the 'voice in my head' is not who I am. 'Who am I then?' The one who sees that."

~Eckhart Tolle

"Ultimately you are not a person, but a focal point where the universe is becoming conscious of itself."

~Eckhart Tolle

"I am who I am in the eyes of God – nothing more and nothing less."

~Richard Rohr

"Thou art that"

Also, "That thou art"…"

~Tat Tvam Asi"

Referred to as a Mahavakya. It is from the Sanskrit pronouncements of Vedantic Sanatana Dharma. It refers to the Self in its transcendent, pure primordial state.

"Give up all questions except one: Who am I? After all, the only fact you are sure of is that you are. The 'I am' is certain. The 'I am this' not. Struggle to find out what you are in reality."

~Sri Nisargadatta Maharaj

"The clearer you understand that on the level of the mind you can be described in negative terms only, the quicker you will come to the end of your search and realize your limitless being."

~Sri Nisargadatta Maharaj

"Midnight. No waves, no wind.

The empty boat

Is flooded with moonlight."

~Eihei Dogen

"Instead of setting about saying there is a mind or an ego and I want to kill it, you must begin to seek its source and find that it [the source of ego] does not exist."

~Sri Ramana Maharshi

The path of Self-discovery, Ramana called it vichara, is to constantly inquire, 'Who am I? Who is asking this question? Who is reading? Who is telling time? etc.

"When you discover the Self within you, you discover the Self in every single thing; when you discover the innate innocence in you, you discover the innocence in every single thing. If there remains a place where conscious awareness has not met itself within you, there will be the perception of the experience of something being wrong…"

~Devaji

"…He who is in you is greater than he who is in the world."

~1 John 4:4 *(English Standard Version of the Bible)*

Jesus can be understood to be comparing God, (the "He", the Self) with the personal self (the "he", that is in the world.

"…It is no longer I who live, but it is Christ who lives in me."

~Galatians 2:20 *(New King Jame Version of the Bible)*

Saint Paul can be understood as speaking from a cosmic perspective and referring to the loss of a limited personal perspective.

"In the same way, let your light shine before others, that they may see your good deeds and glorify your Father in heaven."

~Mathew 5:16 *(New International Version of the Bible)*

God, not the self, is the source of all that is good.

"But the most complete Divine Manifestation, surprising as it may seem, is the human reality, this subtle nervous system – a potential expanse of illumination greater than the physical cosmos and greater than the eternal heavenly realms."

~Ramakrishna

"As long as you regard any event or activity in your life, including your physical body, as other than God, your mind will remain divided, and conscious union of shiva and shakti within the nerve channels of the subtle body will be impossible."

~Ramakrishna

A Mirror Exercise: An Experiential Opportunity

If you feel willing and secure enough in your sense of self to try an exercise where your egoic identity may feel temporarily weakened, here is a process you may appreciate.

Looking into a mirror, fix your attention on your eyes or one eye.

Just stay focused on your eye or eyes. Let minutes go by.

You may start to have an experience relating to the insubstantiality of the body.

You might experience your eyes as a passageway to something even more real.

Or, you may have any number of other possible experiences.

The main point is an evolving sense that the body is not the highest reality of who you are.

An Integration

The personal self that appears to be constantly changing is itself, appearance, and not the Self at all. Yet, as we grow and change, there is an underlying Reality. There is an underlying Self. It is there all along. Albeit unseen. Albeit unfelt.

Just as the sun is there on a cloudy day. We are always our Self. Always One with that which Is. It matters not where we are on our journey of Self-remembrance. It matters not what we think or believe.

Our completeness accompanies us every step of the way. It is like a shadow, although it is a shadow of Light. And, at any moment, it may burst through the darkness of the ego to Grace us with Light.

 It is our inmost center, our Greatness. It is everything and nothing. It is our I. And, it is Love. And it floods us with Goodness.

In Essence

We are not who we think we are.

Thinking will never encompass our Divine Nature. Self-Actualization is not an achievement.

We already are our Divine Self.

And while the work takes effort, attention and devotion, Actualization comes, we are told, as a gift beyond our doing.

It is everything, and at the same time, the masters say, the most natural thing there is.

Chapter 3

HEALING THE HURT CHILD WITHIN

The Past Doesn't Go Away by Itself

⸻

The Inner Child lives as a series of memories, primarily held in the unconscious as a result of childhood experiences. Of those childhood memories, those imprinted most deeply are often those that were traumatic.

Our present age is inconsequential. Even exact details are less important than recognizing the intensity of the feelings experienced by the Inner Child at the time of past events. And these feelings may be buried in the unconscious; but, that doesn't stop them from profoundly influencing our life.

This chapter addresses our wounded child, and how to facilitate much-needed healing. Childhood hurts do not expire with time. They are stored invisibly in the body and mind until they receive the proper attention and healing they need. And then we are more able to experience our authentic Best Self.

Because these hurts happened to us so long ago, we may believe that any power they once held over us has vanished. But, the only aspect that has disappeared is *our conscious awareness* of the hurts and not their existence. Their influence is still just as potent.

Regardless of our age, there are powerful and viable ways to bring healing to our wounded child within, which we will explore in this chapter. However, one thing is certain; to heal will require our attention, Love and perseverance.

Self-Inquiry Questions

- Are you willing to explore the pain of the past in order to free yourself from it?
- Are you trying to protect or blame your parents for the emotions you are carrying?
- Are you willing to re-parent yourself?
- Can you Love parts of yourself that you have been judging?

Quotes About the Importance of Healing the Wounded Child

"Every time we're in touch with the experience of suffering, we believe we can't bear it, and we stuff our feelings and memories deep-down in our unconscious mind. But, just because we may have ignored the Child doesn't mean she or he isn't there. The wounded child is always there, trying to get our attention."

~Thich Nhat Hanh

"The cry we hear from deep in our hearts comes from the wounded Child within. Healing this inner child's pain will transform negative emotions."

~Thich Nhat Hanh

"The truth about our childhood is stored up in our body…But someday our body will present its bill…and it will not stop tormenting us until we stop evading the truth."

~Alice Miller

"We are, in a sense, our own parents, and we give birth to ourselves by our own free choice of what is good."

~St. Gregory of Nyssa, Bishop

A Summary of All That I Have Learned

Over the last 30 years, I have developed a form of Inner-Child healing that plays a central part in the work I now call 'Awakening Greatness'. I may have done close to 25,000 client sessions that included Inner-Child work. By all reports, the results have been strikingly positive.

1. The unconscious is like a basement. Anything experienced in your life, whether positive or negative, is still in that basement, making an impact. You have a choice to heal and clear out the unwanted residual effects.

2. It doesn't matter how long ago the experience or impact occurred. ***THERE IS NO PAST IN THE <u>UNCONSCIOUS</u>.*** Everything exists as 'now', not as 'then'; so, the suggestion to "just get over it" is not a realistic option.

3. The mind of the child is inherently narcissistic; it's a built-in survival mechanism to protect the developing self. Everything that happens to a child, usually up until the age of six or seven, is held in the child's unconscious mind as being about them.

4. If the mother or father were unloving, absent, cruel, abusive, etc., the child can't help but believe that they deserve to be unloved or abused. Unless these embedded beliefs are healed, they will continue to be acted out through life.

5. The good news is that because there is no time sense in the unconscious, you can, in this moment, give your Inner Child the Love, care, and protection they did not get, but desperately needed.

6. There is not just one big Inner Child. The so-called Inner Child is in fact a significant number of individual emotion-filled memories that are available for interaction and healing.

7. The number and intensity of the Inner Child memories will be in direct proportion to how long the painful and traumatic events continued in childhood. For simplicity's sake, we call each of these memory-moments, collectively, the Inner Child.

8. The cumulative effect of these experiences has an ongoing and profound influence on how we function as adults, just as Wordsworth so poetically writes in the first of the next group of quotes.

Quotes About Getting to Know Your Inner Child

"The Child is father of the Man."

~William Wordsworth

"Caring for your inner child has a powerful and surprisingly quick result: Do it and the child heals."

~Martha Beck

"We tend to often tend to ignore how much of a child is still in all of us."

~Elisabeth Kübler-Ross

"Most survivors grew up too fast. Their vulnerable child-selves got lost in the need to protect and deaden themselves. Reclaiming the inner child is part of the healing process."

~Laura Davis

"Research shows that being in touch with your inner child is healing…Only by loving and healing our inner child can we begin to love ourselves and then, consequently, others."

~Diana Raab, Ph.D.

"For your inner child to come out of hiding, he must be able to trust that you will be there for him."

~John Bradshaw

What Does It Mean To Heal the Inner Child?

 Each Inner Child moment has an individual and unique personality which has its own desires, needs, and specific things they will do or allow at each moment. This often is quite surprising to the person experiencing it for the first time. One client exclaimed, "Oh, my God! There really is someone there!"

The willingness and ability to accurately assess the specific needs and receptivity of the Inner Child in the moment of healing is important. Trust must be established by giving the Child the 5A's (see Chapter 1), with no agenda other than honoring what is happening for the Child and what the Child needs.

You don't have to believe me…why not explore it for yourself?

Part 1: Making the Connection

You can connect with an Inner Child moment by either remembering a painful event from childhood, or by tuning into a painful emotion…that is active for you now.

1. Imagine that the pain is being felt by your Inner Child. Remember, feelings are the key, not the actual details. Running the particulars over and over in your mind will not lead to healing. Addressing the Inner Child's feelings with kindness and caring will open the door to healing.

2. Take the role of a proactive Loving Adult who has come to protect and care for the Child, who is separate from you.

3. Say something like the following to open the door to interaction with the Child as we began to do in the Love chapter:

   a. "Hi, I've come to be with you.

   b. Ask, "Would it be OK if I sat beside you?"

   c. Say, "You have the right to feel whatever you're feeling and still be cared for, still be loved."

If these words don't work for you, feel free to change them to loving/supportive words that do work for you.

1. After a while, check-in with the Child. Do you get a feeling of, "Yes," or "No?"

Give the Child full permission to be just as they are, and to say "no" if they want.

Give them full Allowing.

2. Continue to communicate with the Child and ask them what they want. Would the Child like to hold your hand? Sit in your lap? Have your arm around their shoulder? Would the Child like a hug or would that be too much for them?

Many people realize that they can actually tell what the Child will or won't allow at each step.

3. If all is going well, imagine spending 30 minutes to an hour with the Child doing whatever they want. Take one or two minutes to envision how the Child is responding.

4. Now, look to see if the Child has changed in any way as a result of this little bit of Love.

Remember that you're holding in your mind and heart that this time of Child-tending has passed.

Here is a key: the unconscious can't tell the difference between real and imagined. So as you imagine an hour passing, your Inner Child will get the benefit of an hour of Love. Even though it's only been a minute or two.

1. Now, imagine a whole day.

    a. feel your care/Love for the Child – this is central to the healing.

    b. Imagine a day of giving that Love.

2. Now, look to see if the Child has changed.

Quotes About Healing the Inner Child

"Your wish to change your childhood has been granted."

~Cathryn Taylor

If you wish it, and you're willing to do the inner work, it isn't too late for a happy childhood.

"Usually hidden under our grown-up personas, the Inner Child holds the key to intimacy in relationships, physical and emotional well-being, recovery from addictions and the creativity and wisdom of our inner selves."

~Lucia Capacchione

"Of course, there is not a literal child inside you; however, there is a part of your mind that is still caught up in the drama and chaos and pain of your childhood."

~Doreen Virtue

"Our inner child gives us direct access to our subconscious beliefs and we can teach our inner child new healthy life affirming beliefs."

~Rachel Hope

"If we do not work on all three levels – body, feeling, mind – the symptoms of our distress will keep repeating the story stored in its cells until it is finally listened to and understood…The more we idealize the past and refuse to acknowledge our childhood sufferings, the more we pass them on unconsciously to the next generation."

~Alice Miller

Where the Healing Leads

We humans were given a very important gift through the workings of the subconscious: the ability to hide and suppress emotions that are unbearable and cannot be dealt with at the time. In childhood, we are virtual prisoners in the house of our caregivers or parents.

If there is abuse, and/or if there is serious and continuing pain, at age 3, 5, or even 9 and older, the child's mind is incapable of handling it. And so, it suppresses what is intolerable, and places it in the subconscious until a time comes when

1. It is safe to deal with what was not safe before; or

2. We get fed up with the same painful issues from childhood coming up again and again.

3. We get fed up with marrying aspects of our parents.

For most of us, we will do nothing until the pain and frustration become too intense; or, as Alice Miller writes, we want to protect our children from our unconscious negative behavior. The famous psychoanalyst Carl Jung highlights the importance of this when he wrote: "Nothing has a stronger influence psychologically on their environment and especially their children than the unlived life of the parent."

And God knows, the unhealed rage, hate, depression, fear, and judgment is central to the unlived life of the parents.

So what can we do about these Inner Child moments? As Jung would say, the cumulative effect of similar Inner Child moments combines to create a complex pattern.

Let's say that as a result of childhood neglect, you have a habit of thinking of yourself as not being good enough. Think of this pattern as a mosaic comprised of hundreds of little tiles. Every time we clear away one of those tiles, one of those moments, it is as if we are standing right up against the mosaic and looking through the open space where the tile was.

What we experience in that open space is what I would call our Best Self. It is the place where our Goodness resides. If you use the word God, it is the place where the God-given qualities of our Goodness exist undistorted.

And, for a short time, we recognize who we really are. We are the Good, not the blocks that obscure the Good. But soon, we will step back, and then we will be aware of the pattern and not the space we opened in the pattern. It is easy then, to forget that we have done something that is permanently valuable. The tile is gone, the egoic memory bubble has popped. And, I believe it has popped forever.

But, there is still a great deal of work to do to free ourselves from the pattern. More clearing needs to be done. It really is like going to the gym. Working out one time won't make a new muscle. It takes repetition. And, it is the same for freeing ourselves from patterns.

What does it feel like when a tile or bubble is gone? Follow these steps, and you might get a surprising and quite wonderful answer.

Part 2: Growing Up the Child

If, as your Loving Adult, you've spent an imagined day with your hurt child (as described above), imagine giving that child care and protection for an imagined week.

1. Feel the care; imagine a week of such care and protection and check-in to see how the Child has responded.

   a. If all is going well, imagine a month of that Love.

   b. Look to see how the Child is doing.

If you can't imagine the Child benefiting from your care and protection, then it is too soon to do this part of the process. You might just stay with offering care and protection while expecting nothing from the Child. This only works when the Child is feeling loved, protected, and is ready to start growing up.

2. Next, check-in with the Child about how much feels right to help the Child jump forward in time…perhaps six months or a year. Do this process every time: feel the loving care and desire to protect (this is essential for it is this Love that is healing).

3. Imagine a period of time has passed, and check to see how the Child has responded after this time has passed. A central element of this process is that you use your imagination to determine how *this* Child is doing as a result of receiving Love.

   a. *Remember, it won't work if you imagine yourself at that time.*

4. Imagine this Child at various times as you continue to Love and protect and care for him or her: first grade, first date, with friends, graduating high school, additional education or work, serious relationships, perhaps marriage and kids. Then at some maturity level, maybe 30 or 40 years, ask yourself: what qualities do I sense in this person?

5. Imagine writing a list of wonderful qualities. This is You with the hurt gone! This is an aspect of you, a facet of the diamond

of your Best Self. It will never be lost. There are many facets waiting to be uncovered. However, when you take your awareness off of this newly awakened aspect of you, it may *seem* forgotten or lost.

Sometimes it may take many clearings before a change will show up in our life experience; however, this is not always the case.

There was a man, who as a child was given money, but not Love. This resulted in resentment towards money and resistance to earning it as an adult. As a result of connecting with this inner child and giving him Love, within hours of this exercise, he received two offers of lucrative work.

Additional Supportive Exercises

Exercise 1:

Thich Nhat Hanh suggests that you breathe in and say, "I go back to my inner child," and breathe out and say, "I take care of my inner child."

Exercise 2:

This exercise may help you get in touch with the Inner Child's feelings.

Explore your inner Child's feelings by imagining the hurt, angry, sad, or alone Child and writing out what she or he wants to say. Perhaps, you can then have someone read the letter to you.

An Integration

The stunning beauty and radiance of all the facets of your Best Self are waiting to be uncovered. There is nothing that is not beautiful and divine waiting for your healing attention to allow it to shine forth.

Love lies waiting. Creativity is waiting to bubble forth, as is Infinite Wisdom, and Abundance...which is your nature.

One of the most powerfully distorting shadows that live in your unconscious are the wounds from childhood. Time does not erase them. Hiding them is impossible, and it will do no good.

The shadows call out for healing. They have the voice of your Inner Child. They cry out for Love, caring, and protection. They wait for you to heal them...and only you can do so.

The shadows are like clouds that obscure the Sun. This Sun is your Divine Nature. And, when the clouds are gone, and the wounds are healed, the experience will be absolutely glorious.

In Essence

There is no past in your unconscious.

Everything is stored as now.

All of the hurts are there.

All of the limiting beliefs you held are still there.

The hurts and misperceptions act as if they were happening now.

The good news is that because there is no past in the unconscious, you can give yourself the Love, attention and wisdom that you hadn't received then.

The result of this will be the healing of the hurt child within.

Chapter 4

FORGIVENESS OR GRIEVANCE

A Heaven or a Hell of Your Choosing

O ur egos cannot help feeling anger, resentment and even hate; but, we are not our egos, and we don't have to live in our egoic emotions. We have a True Self - a Soul whose nature is Great-Love. Forgiveness helps us to grow beyond the helpful but limited mental perspective of being a creator of our life experience.

Forgiveness is a direct path to letting go of the past and to opening up our hearts. By giving attention, acceptance, and compassion to our hurting and wounded emotions, we can transform them into forgiveness and move beyond grievances.

Without forgiveness we will live, consciously or unconsciously, in a self-created hell of judgment, pain, recriminations, sorrow and regret; however, we don't have to remain in this egoic state where Great-Love is excluded.

I hope you will find value in distinguishing between egoic forgiveness and Authentic Forgiveness, which helps liberate the soul. Without Authentic Forgiveness, we lock up part of our heart in judgment and a cave of the past.

Self-Inquiry Questions

- Can you experience a difference between egoic-forgiveness and deep-forgiveness?
- What would you lose if you forgave?
- What would you gain?
- Can you Love and at the same time blame?

Quotes About the Wisdom of Forgiveness

"What could you want that forgiveness cannot give?

Do you want peace? Forgiveness offers it.

Do you want happiness, a quiet mind, a certainty of purpose, and a sense of worth and beauty that transcends the world?

Do you want care and safety, and the warmth of sure protection always?

Do you want a quietness that cannot be disturbed, a gentleness that never can be hurt, a deep, abiding comfort, and a rest so perfect it can never be upset.

All this, forgiveness offers you."

~A Course in Miracles

"It is as sure that those who hold grievances will forget who they are, as it is certain that those who forgive will remember."

~A Course in Miracles

"The mark of your ignorance is the depth of your belief in injustice and tragedy. What the caterpillar calls the end of the world the master calls a butterfly."

~Richard Bach

"All wrongdoings arise in the mind. It is through the mind that wrongdoings can disappear."

~Thich Nhat Hanh

Peter asked Jesus if he should forgive up to seven times. Jesus answered, "I tell you, not just seven times, but seventy-seven times!"

~Matthew, 18:22 (*New International Version of The Bible*)

"The fundamental mood of the ego: never forgive, never forget."

~Ken Wilber

"All are forgiven – moreover, dears, no one has ever been guilty."

~Kabir, (*Translated by Daniel Ladinsky*)

"Who takes vengeance or bears a grudge acts like one who, having cut one hand while handling a knife, avenges himself by stabbing the other hand."

~Jerusalem Talmud, Nedarim 9:4

"The practice of forgiveness is our most important contribution to the healing of the world."

~Marianne Williamson

"When unresolved issues are writing our life story, we are not our own autobiographers; we are merely recorders of how the past continues, often without our awareness, to intrude upon our present experience and shape our future directions."

~Daniel J. Siegel, M.D., and Mary Hartzell, M.Ed.

Egoic Forgiveness

To our egos, grievances, resentments, and grudges are natural, especially in the early stages of its growth. As the ego matures, sharing and caring, and letting things go are perceived to be of deeper value. A phrase that describes the ego is "what's in it for me?" The ego may appear to act with generosity, but its goal would be to look good and to not actually be generous.

The ego is our limited self-identity. It is who we think we are when we say "I," as opposed to who we are as a manifestation of the Divine. It experiences itself as separate, and is always looking out for itself and its best interest. Because the ego experiences itself as separate, and has its identity in being separate, anything that causes it to lose its boundaries and begin to feel united is perceived to be a threat.

Forgiveness dissolves boundaries. This is why the visionary Ken Wilber says that the fundamental mood of the ego is never to forgive.

To the ego, anything that did not go its way can create a grievance. If the ego feels powerless, especially in childhood, it may immediately push this grievance into the unconscious. It will suppress the grievance to avoid the pain of feeling the hurt or the danger of acting on it. These grievances and resentments will pile up until there is enough safety to give them expression.

At that time, someone or something will trigger the suppressed grievances, and they will come pouring out and add to an upset that has served as the trigger.

The ego cannot truly offer forgiveness because true forgiveness has its basis in Love, which comes from our Divine nature. So the egoic forgiveness it gives cannot bring peace or healing. It is, in essence, just a ploy to make the ego feel better.

A Look at Four Forms of Egoic Forgiveness

1. **Forgiveness through Condemnation.** The ego knows a superficial form of forgiveness, the purpose of which is to make the ego feel good about itself. An example of egoic forgiveness is seen in a person who says they forgive someone for saying something derogatory by saying, "I forgive them, they are such a limited person, you never know what could escape from their mouth." This is egoic forgiveness through condemnation.

2. **Forgiveness through Superiority.** Egoic forgiveness through superiority can be found in an offer of forgiveness so that the forgiver can feel superior. Someone might say, "Oh yes, I've forgiven them. It's a trivial thing, and I'm better than that." Or, even by pretending not to be bothered by something said or done. Or, by saying but not feeling the equivalent of, "We Christians forgive."

3. **Forgiveness through Unconsciousness.** In this, the ego hardens or numbs itself to actions or statements it resents; and when that event happens, it doesn't register it consciously. But, resentment can be seething unconsciously. So the seeming forgiver can say and even think they mean, "It doesn't bother me at all, so there is no need for forgiveness."

4. **Forgiveness through Mandate.** And, finally, there is God-mandated egoic forgiveness. In this, our religion or philosophical perspective tells us we have to forgive. We try not to judge out of fear of judgment. Perhaps, we even pretend. We've got the teaching in our heads, but not in our hearts, so it is superficial, and we may often feel guilty at our limited success. This is spiritualized egoic forgiveness.

While we may often, or even always think of ourselves as our egoic personality, the Masters tell us we are actually Divinity having a human experience. At the core, we are Divine, and all the qualities of the Divine exist within us.

Grievance holds us in ego and limitation. True forgiveness connects us with the Divine within. When we are Divinely connected, we experience joy, compassion, generosity, brilliance, creativity, and all of the other flavors of God expressed in humanity. To settle for egoic forgiveness is such a loss of a great opportunity.

The Wisdom of Forgiveness (Continued)

"Always forgive your enemies – nothing annoys them so much."

~Oscar Wilde

"Forgiveness is not the misguided act of condoning irresponsible, hurtful behavior. Nor is it a superficial turning of the other cheek that leaves us feeling victimized and martyred. Rather it is the finishing of old business that allows us to experience the present, free of contamination from the past."

~Joan Borysenko

"He who is devoid of the power to forgive is devoid of the power to love."

~Martin Luther King, Jr.

"In forgiveness, the salt of bitterness becomes the salt of wisdom."

~Carl Jung

"When a deep injury is done us, we never recover until we forgive."

~Alan Paton

"Inner peace can be reached only when we practice forgiveness. Forgiveness is letting go of the past, and is therefore the means for correcting our misperceptions."

~Gerald Jampolsky

Forgiveness means giving up all thoughts for a better past.

~Anonymous

There are many variations of this quote from Anne Lamott, Rev. Don Felt, John A. MacDougall, Gerald G. Jampolsky, Gina Berriault, Dorothy Bullitt and Lily Tomlin.

"Neuroscience now shows us that we attach to negativity like 'Velcro' unless we intentionally develop another neural path like forgiveness or letting go."

~Richard Rohr

"Forgiveness is for yourself because it frees you. It lets you out of the prison you put yourself in."

~Louise Hay

"Genuine forgiveness does not deny anger but faces it head-on."

~Alice Miller

Growing in True Forgiveness

Heartfelt forgiveness has a spiritual basis, and like all spiritual growth, it unfolds. It is rarely complete at its beginning. Its first step is the genuine desire to forgive. A first step may come from the pain we feel in judging, resenting, or hating, and the desire to get out of that pain. Or, perhaps it may come from those who seek guidance and respond to the teachings of Jesus, Buddha, or the late Rebbe, Menachem Schneerson, to name a few.

In reading the words of these teachers, we want to follow their guidance. Often the authentic desire to forgive in this first stage is mixed, even within minutes, with the ego's craving for revenge, punishment, or self-justification. And so, as not to lose our growing desire to forgive, we need a consistent source of inspiration, like friends, books, or teachers.

The intellect can support a step towards forgiveness by helping the heart feel safe to take this path. The mind can remind us that we live in what can be called "classroom earth". No one in this classroom, save a few masters perhaps, are considered perfected humans. We are all here to learn and grow, and that means we all make mistakes.

In the earlier earth classrooms, our mistakes were more grievous. If you accept that many lifetimes contribute to our advancement, then these mistakes in no way mean that you are a bad person, only that you are growing like the rest of us.

If we embrace the Classroom Earth perspective, we can expand this idea to include that we attract people to help us learn and grow – regardless of whether or not they bring seemingly good or bad things. It can be empowering to choose to believe that the deliverer of a seemingly bad thing has been "hired" by us to deliver a growth opportunity. Oprah Winfrey puts it this way: "True forgiveness is when you can say 'Thank you for that experience.'"

More Wisdom of Forgiveness

"Forgiveness is a choice, but it is not an option."

~Joel Osteen

"Forgiveness liberates the soul, it removes fear. That's why it's such a powerful weapon."

~Nelson Mandela

"Forgive others not because they deserve forgiveness, but because you deserve peace."

~Jonathan Lockwood Huie

"A happy marriage is the union of two good forgivers."

~Ruth Bell Graham

An Experience From My Practice

Is it possible to forgive too quickly? The truth is Yes. If we are filled with anger or resentment, releasing the anger or emotional charge must be done first. If not, forgiveness will be superficial, and the underlying emotions will linger.

One technique that has helped my clients release the emotional charge that restricts forgiveness is called "The Virtual Reality Room".

In this Process, you imagine a room created for healing, where nothing you do or think could hurt anyone because its purpose is healing. In this room, you can imagine and visualize anything that can help you express and release pent-up anger.

Imagine you can stamp, shout, smash things, blow things up, throw bombs - even blow up the world. The key is to find a visual that most closely matches your anger and stay with that imagined activity until the emotion is reduced or spent.

For example, if you're furious, kicking a can or shouting "darn" won't work. It must be a match to your anger.

One of my clients said this about the Virtual Reality Room: "I wouldn't have believed it if I hadn't experienced it…it seemed like decades of anger and frustration was pouring out…like somehow I had opened a hidden volcano and felt the energy pour out of me, burn up the world and then, somehow disappear.

On the one hand, it felt like I was releasing for ages. Yet, this whole experience lasted only five or six minutes. After it was over, I felt like a different person and that an incredibly heavy burden was gone. I have used the Virtual reality Room now, many times…each time with profound results." -B. Dallas, TX

A Forgiveness Process

1. Think of a person with whom you would like to enter into forgiveness, and then reflect on the critical points of what they may or may not have done or withheld from you, as well as the critical points of what you may or may not have done or withheld from them. It is important to try to include their perspective of what may have happened.

2. Imagine, and call forth the Higher Self of the other person. This part of them sees and knows that everything that occurs in our lives offers us a chance for growth and healing. You cannot fail to be forgiven for anything if you connect with this part of them.

3. Find within yourself any sadness, guilt, remorse, or shame you may feel for anything that has occurred between you.

4. Say to the Higher Self, "I am sorry for any harm, real or imagined that I have done to you."

5. Open to feel if this knowing and loving Higher Self accepts your apology and remorse.

6. Invite your Higher Self to support you in your intention to forgive the other person.

7. Say to that person, "And I am open to forgive you for anything, real or imagined, that you might have done to me."

8. "I choose to see all that occurred as an opportunity for my growth in this lifetime."

9. Imagine your Higher Selves embraced in Love; and, if it feels appropriate, imagine that you and the other person at the level of the body embrace or shake hands.

I have seen this Process have very real outcomes in our day-to-day reality, even if it may seem ephemeral to you.

An Integration

Bring into the dark, remote regions of your anger and hate, the white Light of forgiveness and Love. For nothing can resist the Light of God.

Darkness melts in the Light, for darkness secretly yearns for the Light, yearns to be free.

Give over your hurts and pains. Let them go. Do you really wish to carry them any further than you need?

Do not hold others as the source of your pain. This focus of your rage is not what harms you.

It is you who have drawn them. It is you who have created them. It is you who can let them go.

The anger only dims your Light.

I forgive you because you have done nothing. I forgive you because I am the creator. I forgive you because you are simply my teacher.

In the Light of forgiveness, darkness slips into nothingness, and only peace remains.

In Essence

We can live in judgment, or we can live in Love.

The choice is ours to make.

And, if we desire a life lived in peace, happiness, and empowerment, then we will want to choose a life lived in Love.

To realize such a life requires forgiveness.

Forgiveness is an active process.

It requires our attention, devotion, and commitment.

It may just be the most valuable thing we ever do.

Chapter 5

THE CREATOR PERSPECTIVE

Choosing Empowerment over Victimization

W hat if all the events of your life actually help you to grow and create a more positive future?

Do we attract, manifest, or create the events and circumstances in our lives?

Do we choose our parents, our family and our birth; or, are we born with limited, or no control in a world where events just happen to us?

Are we creators or victims, and is there any way to tell for sure? Probably not. In the end, our decision will come down to belief.

By choosing to embrace positive or negative beliefs, we develop a perspective, a worldview, and there are very impactful outcomes. We tend towards depression and hopelessness if we live a life in which we act from a victim's perspective. Accumulated resentments negatively affect our health, our emotions and our relationship with God. All this and more are the result of living from a powerless perspective.

On the other hand, we can choose to embrace the idea that all that happens to us is a purposeful and valuable part of our Soul's journey.

From this perspective, life is a classroom, and we see events as opportunities for growth and evolution. This perspective allows us to accept what is, and to participate in our lives as creators of the next moment.

Creators of our future or victims of the past, which do you choose? You do have a choice!

Self-Inquiry Questions

- Is your current life focused on powerlessness and weakness or empowerment and positivity?
- Are you willing to become more conscious of your thoughts?
- Are you subconsciously trying to punish yourself for things in the past?
- Do you believe in a punishing God or a loving God?

The Power in Choosing the Creator Perspective

"I am responsible for what I see. I choose the feelings I experience, and I decide upon the goal I would achieve. And everything that seems to happen to me I ask for, and receive as I have asked."

~A Course In Miracles

"All that we are is a result of what we have thought."

~Buddha

"Our life is what our thoughts make it."

~Marcus Aurelius

"Until you make the unconscious conscious, it will direct your life and you will call it fate."

~Carl Jung

Our Reality Is Our Creation

What we tell ourselves regarding an event is directly connected to how we feel about the event. For example, let's say you are holding a door open for someone to enter a building who walks through, paying no attention to you without saying "thank you."

You might feel angry, and you might want to say sarcastically, "you're welcome your majesty." And, if you did, you would likely feel resentment or anger.

But, what if you told yourself that you were holding the door open because you choose to engage in acts of kindness because it feels good to you? How would you feel then? Would it really matter if the person did not receive your gift?

Can you see, in this example, how you choose to regard a situation as being responsible for your feelings?

Try a Visualization With Me

1. Imagine that bad, painful, cruel things happen to you in a world where no one cares, and you are powerless to protect yourself. And, everything is happening for no purpose at all. How do you feel?

2. Imagine that even if bad, painful, or cruel things happened to you, you saw purpose in them. And, you believed that everything would eventually make you more capable of accessing the great power, Love, and wisdom of your Best Self. How would you feel living with this perspective?

No one can prove that either perspective is true. So if you choose to embrace the growth perspective, you don't have to defend it as the Truth. You can simply say, "I choose to believe this, and it works for me."

Nurturing the Path of Creatorship

"What seems to be in the way is the way."

~David Richo

"If you want to see what your unconscious is programmed to create, look at your life now and then you can say, 'Oh, this is what I think I want."

~Rick Moss

"All states of mind reproduce themselves…the universe is just a big Xerox machine. It simply produces copies of your thoughts.

~Neal Donald Walsch

"Stop creating your own reality. It isn't working."

~Dr. Jacob Lieberman

" If you find yourself in a hole, stop digging."

~Will Rogers

The Power of the Unconscious in Our Creatorship

As Dr. Bruce Lipton points out in his book *"The Honeymoon Effect"*, it's more than clear that we are not creating a life exactly as we want with our conscious mind. This is not surprising when we consider that the conscious mind is in charge about 5% of the time. The conscious mind can perform about seven tasks per second, while the unconscious is a million times more powerful.

To give you a sense of the power of the unconscious, imagine that you are walking down a street. You sense that you are interested in a person walking to your left. You turn to look. Before you see that person, your unconscious has compared that person's face against everyone you have ever seen, and has positively weighted your favorable reactions.

In fact, before you can see this person, your mind has already told you whether or not you are attracted to them.

To further understand the unconscious' power and nature, the unconscious retains every experience and thought you have ever had. And, the thoughts that have emotions connected to them have a greater impact than facts. So, for example, the thought, 'no one loves me' has a tremendous emotional charge.

This thought and its emotional charge will profoundly affect your interpretation of an event in which it might appear that you are not loved. And, not only that, but it is likely to attract similar events to you in the future.

A belief system will tend to reproduce itself. The unconscious searches for belief validation, and it causes us to seek out people that will validate our negative self-assessment. And, too often, our unconscious would rather be right than happy.

Freud described this as part of a pattern he called 'Repetition Compulsion'. I believe that we see the validity of this compulsion in the common understanding that some people marry a person who reminds them of their parents, and what things were like when they were a child, regardless of whether it was unloving or abusive or not.

How Are Belief Systems Created?

If you accept the possibility of past lives, then let's begin there.

In the 30-plus years I have done this work, I have seen many phobias and troublesome mental states eliminated or greatly reduced through what I call 'Life Story Clearing.' A client does not have to believe in past lives to investigate whether their unconscious holds a story that has a negative outcome that may affect their daily lives.

Here is a rather dramatic example (with some minor facts altered to protect the client's identity): A woman working in the field of law had been depressed with suicidal tendencies since she was 18. As I used intuition to track the story she was holding in her unconscious mind, I was led to a story of her as a mother in the times of Aztec sacrifices in Central America. In her unconscious story, she was forced to give up her child to be sacrificed. She was 18. And the moment she gave up her child, she went into traumatic shock and deep depression.

When she turned 18 in this life, the unconscious story was activated and started working its way towards consciousness. I could see that she was very intuitive and sensitive, and I asked her to go into consciousness and find the child's Soul. She said that she had. I then asked her to ask the child if it came in to be sacrificed, because this was the fastest and least painful way to move through the karma of killing someone in a previous life.

The child confirmed this and thanked the mother for her unconscious willingness to provide her with this great gift of liberation. The woman cried and cried, and when she finished, she smiled. My understanding is that the depression and suicidal thoughts went away from that day.

I have facilitated the release of hundreds of what I believe were past-life experiences. Sometimes many past-life experiences contribute to a phobia, or a contracted, negative mental state in this life. Sometimes there is just one. But when the story is released, and an understanding of how this past-life experience has contributed to one's growth, it is easier to move on in this life and leave the trauma behind.

Childhood is a second way that a negative belief system is created. As already mentioned, the first six to seven years are the most impactful. The child's mental ability is limited, and the child will only be able to think that they are responsible for everything that is happening to them. If the events were damaging, the child will accept a negative conclusion such as 'I'm not good enough', and will very likely push most of the trauma into the unconscious.

I have seen so many clients that have little or no memory of their earlier years. They have just used the unconscious as a storage facility, because they could not examine what they pushed into the storage to stay functional. As an adult, it is safe to go into the storage room and start to clean it out. Now, there is an adult within them to face and heal the childhood pain. Now, a negative belief that they are not good enough can be changed. Now, the Best Self can tell a different story.

Embracing Creatorship

"Everything is by Divine Providence…Every single thing a person sees or hears is an instruction to him in his conduct and service of God."

~Rabbi Israel ben Eliezer

"What we are not changing, we are choosing."

~David Richo

"Not as it was in childhood, but as it is now in unadorned Reality."

~Rick Moss

"This being human is a guest house.

Every morning a new arrival.

A joy, a depression, a meanness,

some momentary awareness comes

as an unexpected visitor.

Welcome and entertain them all!

Even if they're a crowd of sorrows,

who violently sweep your house

empty of its furniture,

still, treat each guest honorably.

He may be clearing you out

for some new delight.

The dark thought, the shame, the malice,

meet them at the door laughing,

and invite them in.

Be grateful for whoever comes,

because each has been sent

as a guide from beyond."

~Rumi *(Translated by Coleman Barks)*

How Can We Come To Trust That What Is Happening to Us Is in Our Best Interest?

Here is a Helpful Visualization:

1. Imagine a person, or an animal, or something in nature that you Love. (If Love is too challenging a word, then someone or something you care deeply about, towards whom you feel kindly.)

2. Ask yourself if while you have those positive feelings, could you purposely harm that person, animal or thing? I think you will agree that when you feel Love or deep caring, you cannot intentionally harm and that Love and harm at the same time are impossible.

3. As yourself, if we cannot even imagine harming and loving simultaneously, could the Creator of Love harm us? Certainly, the Creator of Love must Love at least as much as we do and certainly not less.

4. Imagine, or tune into your feelings as a loving parent and then ask, wouldn't you want your child to have all the resources they need to grow and mature? And, if God or Source, or Spirit *(whatever name works for you)* is our Creator, our True Parent, could you not imagine that the same would be true for our Creator?

If this thinking is true, then it makes sense that our growth must take place over many lifetimes.

And, what seems harmful and unfair to us may be part of the learning that is taking place through lifetimes of experience.

We'll take up this idea more thoroughly when we discuss the concept of Classroom Earth.

I want to share one of those fantastic, but true stories regarding this chapter. There was a glitch as I finished typing the "Quest House" by Rumi. The whole chapter disappeared. In shock and unable to retrieve it, I went to tell my wife. As I told her what happened in the 'Creator Perspective' chapter, I had to laugh…just too unbelievable. This had never happened before.

I realized that I was just going to have to walk my talk! So I said to Robin, "It must mean that I am being asked to do a better job the second time." And, to tell the truth, the second version of this chapter is much improved!

An Integration

The world I see and experience is a product of my mind. When I accept this fact, I am empowered. Everything can be seen as a gift from God, working for my good, even when my ego is incapable of recognizing this.

I am not my ego. I am that expanded awareness untouched by the ego and its beliefs. Let me choose now to be guided by a higher truth, an expanded sense of myself. Let me plant a flag in creatorship.

I choose to embrace the past and be a conscious creator in my future. This choice is mine to make. The pain and shame of being a victim offer nothing to me for the next part of my journey. Yes, I may fall and stumble. But, as a conscious creator, I will not lose my way.

In Essence

How we choose to understand the world, and what we believe have profound consequences in our lives. To hold the perspective of powerlessness and victimization leads to despair and withdrawal.

Accepting everything that has happened to us as essential to our growth, leads to peace of mind and gratitude, instead of resentment.

Realizing that we create our experience in the next moment is empowerment.

Chapter 6

GOD

Spirit, Source, Wholeness,
Divinity, The Absolute, The One

Our intellects cannot comprehend "Him." Our minds cannot contain "Her." Our egos hide from that which is beyond our conscious comprehension.

As we examine our conscious and unconscious resistance to God, we may discover a growing and deepening connection with the Divine and Love itself, and the possibility that God is seeking us.

A heart filled with Love is one with the Divine. When we live in Love continuously, we are God in action.

Self-Inquiry Questions

- How might you explore a God that our limited minds cannot fully comprehend?

- Could you open a space in your awareness for God to communicate with you?

- What might be in the way?

- What other than thought brings you into a feeling of Oneness?

God and the Ego

Nothing I think about God is actually true. The infinite cannot be captured or described in finite words. This has led the ancients to describe God in negative terms. God was described as "not this, not that." Such an approach is called neti neti. However, this negative approach has untenable limitations if one believes that it is all God. This non-dual perspective dates back to the Indian holy books and the Upanishads. To put it succinctly, the Upanishads offer the vision that there is nothing in the universe that is not God.

This vision holds that everything is Good. All of the seeming challenges and problems are means for our spiritual growth and everything that happens to us happens for us.

There are those who believe that God is Good and evil is of the devil. There are those who believe that God and the Soul are good and the ego is not God and not good. In the end, you will make your own decision based on your experience and insight, your teachers and the power of the tradition from which you come.

God and Our Egos

"For my thoughts are not your thoughts, neither are your ways my ways, saith the Lord."

~Isaiah 55:8 *(From the King James Bible)*

"The essence of Vedanta is that there is but one Being and that every soul is that Being in full, not a part of that Being."

~Swami Vivekananda

"In the last resort all we know of God is to know that we do not know Him since we can be sure that the mystery of God surpasses human understanding."

~St. Thomas Aquinas

Because we cannot know what God is, but only what He is not, we cannot consider how He is, but only how He is not.

Be certain that it is impossible God and the ego, or yourself and it, will ever meet.

~A Course in Miracles

"The 19th Century Hasidic rabbi Menachem Mendel Morgenstern of Kotzk once asked some visiting scholars, "Where does God dwell?" They laughed at him and said, "God is everywhere of course." The rabbi shook his head and said, "God dwells wherever man lets him in."

~ The Enlightened Mind *(Edited by Stephen Mitchell)*

"God, whose love and joy are present everywhere, can't come to visit you unless you aren't there."

~Angelus Silesius

"To have faith in God requires that we surrender our ego's belief (demand or desire) that things should be the way it wants them to be."

~Rick Moss

"All separation, every kind of estrangement and alienation is false. All is one."

~Sri Nisargadatta Maharaj

What Is the Ego?

Human growth and development require an evolving ego. The ego is our self-concept and self-creation. It is a collection of our beliefs, memories and past experiences. It is also a repository of the beliefs and projections of others that we have absorbed. It is how we generally answer the question of 'who am I'?

If the ego is severely damaged in early childhood, personal growth can be very difficult, or even seemingly impossible. As the ego matures, it permits, and is open to spiritual growth experiences.

If we stay fixated in our limiting beliefs of who we are, say the great teachers like Yogananda and Ramana Maharishi, this limited awareness of self, the ego, is the source of our problems.

As we mature spiritually, we begin to experience additional aspects of our Being that transcends what we have known and experienced as our-self. These include the capacity for Great Love, spiritual insight, unboundedness, bliss and more.

These abilities and experiences are not of the ego but of the Self. The Self is the identity we share with God.

There are two prominent schools of thought regarding God and the ego. The first is similar to "A Course in Miracles" which holds that the ego is an illusion that exists only in our mind. The second school of thought is non-dualism, as exemplified by Ramakrishna who holds that everything is God, even our self-created identity.

What Is God?

To ask 'what is God' is to pose a question that is unanswerable because words and concepts cannot define the Infinite. At best, we can only offer our minds a provisional working understanding.

Perhaps, we can hold our beliefs and concepts in the light of the profound spiritual metaphor that definitions are like a finger pointing at the moon. The finger is not the moon.

Words in the mind do not reveal God. God is often revealed, however, through experiences in the heart or revelations that transcend the mind. Each revelation and insight brings us closer to a wordless understanding of what is God?

Quotes About God

"If you comprehend it, it is not God."

~St. Augustine

"My me is God."

~St. Catherine of Genoa

"God is the goodness that cannot be wroth, for God is nothing by goodness "

~Mother Juliana of Norwich

"Whoever knows himself knows God."

~Elijah Muhammad

"So it was You all along... Everyone I ever loved–it was You. Everything decent or fine that ever happened to me... Everything that ever made me reach out and try to be better... It was You all along."

~C.S. Lewis

"God is not someone else."

~Thomas Merton

"God comes to us disguised as our lives."

~Paula D'Arcy

"Despair is a denial that there is a God who directs all His creation and watches over every individual and assists each one in what he must accomplish…"

~ Rebbe Menachem Mendel Schneerson

In my breaking through...I transcend all creatures and am neither God nor creature...for in this breaking through I find that God and I are both the same.

~Meister Eckhart

Meister Eckhart wants to help us not grasp onto anything we think is God, but rather push us over the cliff into the Abyss that is God beyond understanding.

Relating, Connecting and Opening to God

As Menachem Mendel Morgensztern of Kotzk said and was quoted above, "God dwells wherever man lets him in." No God can be found to a mind that is closed, too afraid, or invested in its own interpretation of past experiences.

 To a mind that says that there can be no God because of this or that terrible event, spiritual teachers say that God waits with infinite patience for an opening.

How, then, do we let God in? How do we make ourselves available to an experience of God?

When I studied with Maharishi Mahesh Yogi, I remember him saying, "God takes the form that is most pleasing to the aspirant." At the time, I imagined that this was a physical form, like Jesus or an angel; but, over time I have come to believe that the form can also be formless, like Love.

When I observe someone extending Great Love to a person, animal, or nature, I feel like I am in God's presence. I feel holiness. With Love, it is easier for this writer to believe that God's Love is present in this moment and in all moments simultaneously, that it is omnipresent.

Maharishi went on to use the following metaphor to highlight the importance of appreciation in our God-relationship.

"There is a person who loves and is devoted to the artwork of a particular artist. This person knows and loves every work of art the artist has created. The artist, hearing of this devoted enthusiast, comes to shake the hand of the person who loves his creations. Our appreciation of God's creation is an opening to God-relationship."

Sri Ramakrishna Paramahamsa also tells a story illustrating the importance he experienced in both a personal and impersonal relationship with the Divine. Ramakrishna speaks of an advanced, wandering holy man who came to visit him. The holy man convinced Ramakrishna that his devotion to Kali was also his limitation. His fixation on the Goddess Kali restricted his awareness of a transcendent Being.

Following his holy teacher's instruction, Ramakrishna was able to go beyond awareness of the Goddess Kali to the Impersonal God. However, not long after, as his teacher and Ramakrishna sat in the temple, a servant disturbed his teacher, who flew into a rage.

Ramakrishna laughed and pointed out that even with immersion in the transcendent God, he was in the physical world, so easily thrown into a rage. The holy man accepted the teaching and became a devotee of Kali, the personal aspect of God and the more expanded, transcendent God.

This story is an invitation to both a relationship with a personal aspect of God and immersion in an impersonal, transcendent aspect of God.

Maharishi, writing in a little book titled, "Love and God", spoke of the attraction to the devotional relationship with God when he wrote, "Separation for the purpose of devotion is greater still than unity." Perhaps, this separation is but a stage in our ultimate relationship with Oneness.

One thing is for certain, however, the more ego-bound we are, the less room there is for God connection. The more we let the wounds of our hurt inner child dominate our life experience, the less we can open to

Divine awareness. These old inner child hurts are places in our minds that are not open to God.

In the 30-plus years of my experience with this work, I have seen a consistent relationship between a person's pain and trauma with their parents in childhood and their resistance to using the word "God.".

People with similar painful, and traumatic childhood experiences associate God with a negative, raging, narcissistic, or abusive father or mother. It is certainly understandable, but it doesn't have to remain as a closed avenue in our relationship with the word, the concept, or even the experience of God.

To increase our capacity to have a positive child/parent relationship with God, here is a short exercise that might help.

God Is *Not* Your Parents

1. Imagine a child, an animal, or something in nature you feel kind, caring or loving towards.

2. As you feel these positive emotions, ask yourself if you could feel these positive emotions, and still wish to harm that which you are caring for and loving?

I have rarely if ever heard someone say, "Yes.". The response is almost always, "No, I could not feel loving and intend to harm at the same time. I am certain of that!"

1. If, you in your loving state could not harm that which you are loving, how could the Creator of Love love less than you? God must love either equally to your experience of Love or more. Nothing else makes sense.

2. Ask yourself, could you want anything less than all Good for that which you are loving?

3. Now, ask yourself, could God want less for you than you want for that which you Love?

4. So if your parents did harm to you or were unsupportive, they did not love you the way God Loves you. God then, could be thought of as not like your parents but as a Perfect Parent. And this loving, Perfect-Parent-state we can actually find within ourselves in our best moments.

Quotes About Entering into a Relationship With God

"Be still, and know that I am God."

~Psalm 46:10 *(New International Version of the Bible)*

"I have come to learn: God adores His creation."

~Rabia al Basri

"God's Love for you overflows from such a full Heart that it floods the Universe with Light and whispers your name with such tenderness that if your Heart were not Eternal, it would melt."

~Rick Moss

"When you stop looking for God somewhere you will find God everywhere."

~Panache Desai

"Only at the shrine where all are welcome will God sing loud enough to be heard."

~St Teresa of Avila

"If you're feeling further from God than you used to, guess who moved?"

~A sign in front of a church

"Who cares if the world is strewn with thorns? Simply put on sandals and walk over them. The sandals are the knowledge that God alone exists...God is known by ecstatic love, there is no other adequate mode."

~Sri Ramakrishna Paramahamsa

"The sense that one must, or even can, initiate any action begins to disappear as one realizes that only God acts."

~Sri Ramakrishna Paramahamsa

"A seeker can only understand Divine Reality in terms of their own level of inner experience."

~Sri Ramakrishna Paramahamsa

Maharishi Mahesh Yogi spoke of this using the words "knowledge is structured in consciousness"...the level of your consciousness determines the level of your understanding. As our consciousness expands, our understanding and experience of Divine Reality does as well.

"The heart is a sanctuary at the center of which is a little space, wherein the Great Spirit abides, and this is the Eye."

~Sioux Chief Black Elk

"Nibble at me.

Don't gulp me down.

How often is it you have a guest in your house who can fix everything?"

~Rumi (*Translated by Daniel Ladinsky*)

"A good gauge of spiritual health is to write down the three things you most want. If they in any way differ, you are in trouble."

~Rumi (*Translated by Daniel Ladinsky*)

"God is like a magnet constantly reaching out, and our job is to become iron filings."

~Rick Moss

We need to find God, and he cannot be found in noise and restlessness. God is the friend of silence...We need silence to be able to touch souls

~Mother Teresa

"Never lose an opportunity of seeing anything beautiful; for beauty is God's handwriting."

~Ralph Waldo Emerson

"Pray as though everything depends on God. Work as though everything depends on you."

~St. Augustine

"We may ignore, but we can nowhere evade the presence of God. The world is crowded with Him. He walks everywhere incognito."

~C.S. Lewis

"Coincidence is God's way of remaining anonymous."

~Albert Einstein

"Nothing real can be increased except by sharing. That is why God created you."

~A Course in Miracles

"It is only in being open to the unknown, without control, that you find God...In receiving the totality of God's offering, in receiving whatever is up – this is divine connection."

~Devaji

"God comes to shake the hand of the man [person] who appreciates His creation."

~Maharishi Mahesh Yogi

As Rumi and countless other masters have pointed out, if you want one thing and only one thing, then you will have it; want God

Seeking and Deepening Our Connection to God

If we accept that God is real, and if we accept that we live in classroom-earth, and not courtroom earth, then life is about growing and developing and maturing our consciousness, and not about being punished for making mistakes.

If this is classroom-earth then, could the ultimate purpose of everything be to strengthen and deepen our connection and Oneness with God, Buddha Mind, Source, Spirit, Shiva, the Father, Divine Mother, Isness, the Absolute, the Ground State of Being and Hashem?

The question then becomes, how can I use any experience or thought or challenge in classroom-earth to strengthen my God connection? Could it be that in anything that occurs, there is an invitation to come to Wholeness, to connect to God?

Is God Seeking Us?

Could it be that God is actively seeking us? It seems strange to think that an all-powerful Being could be denied anything. But, if free will is actually true, then it must be a God-created possibility. Perhaps, it all makes more sense if we look at the concept that God is our real Parent/Creator.

If you are a parent, think of your most unconditionally loving moments. If you are not a parent, imagine the love you might feel for a child at your most loving moments. In your most loving state of mind, think about missing a child who is not present. Does your heart not yearn for the child?

Can you imagine seeking out that child, inviting the child to come home, and yet not being able to force the child to meet your will? Could it be that God shares a similar parent/child dynamic?

In the Parable of the Prodigal Son (Luke 15:11-32), we read a story Jesus told that indicates the parental nature of God, and illustrates the desire and love the parent has for the child.

In this story, the younger of the two sons wants to leave home. He asks for his inheritance, and wastes it with prodigal living. Having nothing, and starving he decides to return home and live as one of his father's servants. When his father becomes aware that the son is returning home, he greets him with open arms, forgives him and celebrates.

In discussing the Narada Bhakti Sutra (The Aphorisms of Love) Shri Shri Ravi Shankar discusses the flavors of Love and states, "Love blossoms only in longing. If there is no longing, I tell you there is no love also."

He then goes on to tell a story of God as Krishna and his love as Radha. They are young, and walking in the woods, and Krishna asks her to play hide and seek. But, when he can't find her, his longing becomes overpowering and he can't even function. He isn't reunited with her until he closes his eyes and goes within. Then she appears by his side.

So here, we find a parallel to the Biblical story of the Prodigal son. God, as Krishna, longs for that which He loves.

Quotes About How God Yearns for Us

"But, when he was still a great way off, his father saw him and had compassion, and ran and fell on his neck and kissed him"

~Luke 15:20 *(New King James Bible)*

"For this my son was dead, and is alive again; he was lost, and is found."

~Luke 15:24 *(King James Bible)*

"It is a certain truth that God must seek us, as if all his divinity depended on it."

~Rudolf Steiner

Sharing a communication from God. "There is no need to seek. There is no need to look for me….The experience of personal doing, of personal effort, is what prevents me from finding you…It is not a seeking; it is a recognition that there is nothing that I am not. And then my search for you is over. The search is my job, not yours."

~Devaji

"Feel me in the silence and you can know my love for you. Feel me in the fire and you can know my passion for you. Feel me in your cries and you can know I am crying out for you."

~Devaji

An Exercise To Explore the Feeling That God Is Seeking Us

Have you wondered what it would feel like to do nothing but choose to be as still as you can?

1. In your stillness, *be* the seashore, doing nothing but waiting for a wave to come in.

2. When you find your mind wanting to flee the stillness, come back to as much stillness as is available.

3. When you feel some depth to the stillness, see if you can sense that the Ocean of God is seeking the shore of you.

4. Invite the Ocean to cover the shore. Can you sense the intent of the Ocean to reach you? Can you let it?

An Integration

Allowing awareness to drain down out of our heads and fill up our hearts like the sand falling to the lower part of a sand dial, we can move beyond the finite of the intellect into the heart. Our heart knows the infinite when it is in Love.

Just think of someone you Love unconditionally. Like a child. Does this Love have an end? Under any condition?

We are not the creator of this Love. Its Creator is Divine. We are just blessed to be a channel through which it extends into the world.

Yet, when we Love with the heart of God we are most capable to think with the Mind of God.

And we become a worthy servant.

God directs us. And the ego's wishes are nowhere to be found.

We become God in action. And all we are capable of doing is Good.

In Essence

God is beyond our limited understanding but not beyond our feelings.

An open heart embraces everything that is.

As we expand our capacity to Love, we enliven our ability to know the One.

Chapter 7

PRAYER

*Support, Guidance,
Connection On the Way to Union*

———

Prayer at its most fundamental level is our attempt to communicate and connect with God or what we consider a higher power. There are essentially two forms of prayer: praying for something and seeking connection. Praying for something or someone is born out of the ego's sense of need or lack. When there is a pressing need, it's something we've all done, and probably will do again.

Prayer to connect is born out of our innate desire to unite, celebrate, appreciate and be Whole. As we deepen our connection with our Source, it's the direction we will all eventually move towards.

I have spent over 20 years as a minister of Prayer at a Religious Science/New Thought church in California. The focus of my job was to help those present to have an experience that helped them connect with whatever aspect of the Divine that our minister (the brilliant Dr. Bill

Little) was focusing on that day. My work was called an 'Integration'. With visualization, I would often seek to help unite the mental level of understanding with the heart level of experience and feeling. Likewise, I hope to contribute to supporting head/heart integration for you, my reader, and your connection to the Divine.

Self-Inquiry Questions

- Are there limitations in praying for something specific?
- Are you open to exploring new ways to pray?
- What is the connection between gratitude and prayer?
- If it is possible to pray without ceasing, how would that affect your life?

Quotes About Versions of Prayer

"Prayer is the most concrete way to make our home in God."

~Henri Nouwen

"To worship God in order to generate material success or to be victorious in some litigation is not the sign of a true practitioner, who simply opens to whatever gifts of abundance flow spontaneously and mysteriously from Divine Reality."

~Sri Ramakrishna Paramahamsa

"The prayer of religion is petition. The prayer of metaphysics is affirmation. The prayer of mysticism is receptivity to the will of God."

~Joel S. Goldsmith

"Meditation is the highest form of prayer. In it you are so close to God that you don't need to say a thing."

~Swami Chetanananda

"Nothing could bring greater discouragement than to labor under the delusion that God is a Being of moods, who might answer some prayers and not others…God is a Universal Presence, an impersonal Observer, a Divine and impartial Giver, forever pouring Himself into His Creation."

~Ernest Holmes

What Is Prayer?

There are so many divergent ideas as to what constitutes prayer, and yet there is a common component: it is an attempt to connect with something greater than the individual self.

Prayer can be a form of giving thanks or praise. Prayer can take the form of supplication. Many are drawn to prayer as a doorway to communion.

As I was visiting a friend one evening, he went to help his child prepare for bed. I heard his daughter ask him, "Dad, why does God answer some prayers and not others? He responded by saying, "I believe that God is always answering our prayers. But, sometimes the answer doesn't match what we think we want. So when I pray I always finish my prayers with the words, 'this or something greater God', and I let God figure out what is for the best."

More Quotes About Prayer

"You carry Mother Earth within you. She is not outside of you. Mother Earth is not just your environment. In that insight of inter-being, it is possible to have real communication with the Earth, which is the highest form of prayer."

~Thich Nhat Hanh

"Joy is prayer; joy is strength: joy is love; joy is a net of love by which you can catch souls."

~Mother Teresa

"Prayer is a thought, a belief, a feeling, arising within the mind of the one praying."

~Ernest Holmes

"Remember that bodily exercise, when it is well ordered, as I have said, is also prayer by means of which you can please God our Lord."

~Saint Ignatius

"The music that I have learned and want to give is like worshiping God. It's absolutely like a prayer."

~Ravi Shankar

"The desire is thy prayers; and if thy desire is without ceasing, thy prayer will also be without ceasing. The continuance of your longing is the continuance of your prayer."

~St. Augustine

Guidance About How To Pray

Let's focus on the idea that prayer is about connecting with something greater than ourselves. As we all have different backgrounds, beliefs, intentions, and aspirations, there cannot be one style of prayer that is better than another. The real question is, what works best for you?

There are quiet forms of prayer, ecstatic states, meditational approaches, absorption in nature, and guided prayer, to name but a few. But, in my experience, our yearning for connection is our most potent guide.

A famous teaching story emphasizes yearning in which a master is standing in the Ganges River, and a would-be student approaches the master saying, "Master, I want to be your student." The master asks the student to come closer, and pushes the student under the water, and when he finally lets him up, he says to the student, "Now, what do you want?" The student says, "Air!" And the master says, "Then you are not ready." As we grow and evolve, so must our yearning. The yearning will reveal to us how to pray, how to connect.

Quotes About How To Pray

"Prayer is not asking. It is a longing of the soul."

~Mahatma Gandhi

"Our Father who art in heaven, hallowed be thy Name. Thy kingdom come. Thy will be done on earth as it is in heaven. Give us this day our daily bread, and forgive us our trespasses, as we forgive those who trespass against us, and lead us not into temptation, but deliver us from evil. For thine is the Kingdom, and the Power, and the Glory, forever. Amen."

~Jesus to his disciples ("*The Lord's Prayer, Matthew 6:9-13, King James Version*)

"Pray as though everything depended on God. Work as though everything depended on you."

~St Augustine

"Hear, O Israel, the Lord our God, the Lord is One."

~Deuteronomy 6:4 *(New International Version)*

~The Shema Yisrael Jewish prayer

(Observant Jews considered this to be the most important Jewish prayer, and also the first two words of a section of the Torah.)

"I exist

I long

I hope

I trust

I release

I love

I am prepared."

~The Latifa, a Sufi prayer

Sufism is the mystical branch of Islam. Latifa is an ancient Sufi prayer meant to connect us with the essence of our being.

"Om Bhur Bhuva Svah

Tat Savitur Varenyam

Bhargo Devasya Dhimahi

Dhiyo Yo Naha Prachodayat"

On the absolute reality and its planes,

On that finest spiritual light,

We meditate, as remover of obstacles

~The Gayatri Mantra

"In prayer it is better to have a heart without words than words without a heart."

~Mahatma Gandhi

"May I be filled with lovingkindness.

May I be safe from inner and outer dangers.

May I be well in body and happy.

May you be filled with lovingkindness.

May you be safe from inner and outer dangers

May you be well in body and mind.

May you be at ease and happy.

May all beings be filled with lovingkindness.

May all beings be safe from inner and outer dangers.

May all beings be well in body, heart, and mind.

May all beings be at ease and happy."

May all beings everywhere, whether near or far, whether known to me or unknown, be happy.

May they be well. May they be peaceful. May they be free."

~Buddhist Metta Prayer

(Recovery Dharma. This version from Jack Kornfield and Buddha Groove)

"Breathing in, I calm my body.

Breathing out, I smile.

Dwelling in the present moment

I know this is a wonderful moment."

~Thich Nhat Hanh

"For prayer is nothing else than being on terms of friendship with God."

~Saint Teresa of Avila

"For mental prayer in my opinion is nothing else than an intimate sharing between friends; it means taking time frequently to be alone with Him who we know loves us. The important thing is not to think much but to love much and so do that which best stirs you to love. Love is not great delight but the desire to please God in everything."

~Saint Teresa of Avila

"If the only prayer you said was thank you, that would be enough."

~Meister Eckhart

"True prayer is not asking God for love; it is learning to love, and to include all mankind in one's affection. Prayer is the utilization of the love wherewith He loves us."

~Mary Baker Eddy

The Benefits of Prayer

"Prayer does not change God, but it changes him who prays."

~Soren Kierkegaard

"...so the mystic longs for the moment when in prayer he can, as it were, creep into God."

~Soren Kierkegaard

"I deepen my experience of God through prayer, meditation, and forgiveness."

~Marianne Williamson

"I try to remind myself not to go anywhere or do anything without asking for spiritual direction through prayer and meditation."

~Marianne Williamson

"Think of God; attachments will gradually drop away. If you wait till all desires disappear before starting your devotion and prayer, you will have to wait for a very long time indeed."

~Ramana Maharshi

"I don't know whether I believe in God or not. I think, really, I'm some sort of Buddhist. But the essential thing is to put oneself in a frame of mind which is close to that of prayer."

~Henri Matisse

"We should not permit prayer to be taken out of the schools; that's the only way most of us got through."

~Sam Levenson

"When prayer removes distrust and doubt and enters the field of mental certainty, it becomes faith; and the universe is built on faith."

~Ernest Holmes

Why Do We Resist Prayer?

Here is a short list of some of the belief systems of people with whom I've worked. Perhaps some of them may strike a chord with your ego?

Many of these may not be conscious, so explore the thoughts below and wait to see if they stir something within that you can't quite put your finger on or is easily recognized

- I know I'll be disappointed in the end.

- I never get what I want.

- I don't have the right to want more; I don't deserve it.

- God will see that I'm bad and deficient.

- Because of what has happened to me or the world, there can't be a God.

- It is terrifying to encounter something so vast and something I have no control over.

- God is like my father/mother, and I feel too hurt or angry.

- It feels terrifying to be out of control.

Let Us Use Prayer To Take On and Begin To Unwind Some of Our Resistance

Let's work with a generalized definition of prayer as an attempt to connect with something good beyond ourselves. The unconscious is extremely powerful. It manifests what is programmed within it, independent of what the conscious mind believes. This is very much like the functioning of the software in a computer. Applying this idea, if our goal is to open to something new, we have to find a way to create an opportunity to change our minds and especially our unconscious.

A Process

1. Let's use the limiting belief that it is not safe to trust something bigger and more powerful than me. When we were small, we most likely had this feeling.

   a. What is true of the unconscious is: if healing hasn't occurred, an issue is still there no matter how much time has gone by.

2. Say out loud: 'It is not safe to trust something bigger and more powerful than myself'.

   b. Can you find a reaction, a feeling, somewhere in your body? Perhaps it is in your stomach, or your throat tightens?

3. Imagine that this reactive part of your body is in a room, then imagine that you are not in the room, but looking in from the outside.

   a. Use your creative imagination, also called your felt sense, to see or feel into what is in the room. Perhaps it is an animal, a color, maybe a scared child, or perhaps a monster.

4. Imagine that the part of you looking into the room is the kindest, warmest, most caring part of you.

   c. Use the idea that whatever is in the room has been waiting for your positive attention, your Love, to heal. Send the energy of your Caring/Love into the room.

5. Say to whatever is in the room, "You have every right to feel what you feel and still be cared for, still be Loved."

   d. Keep sending that thought and energy. After a while, what is in the room will most likely start changing.

6. Now go into the room with the idea that you are perfectly protected, and say, "I'm here to be on your side, to protect you, to let no harm come to you."

   e. Whatever remains in the room, surround it with your loving-energy arms, but do not touch it. By doing this, you will multiply the power of the healing energy of your heart (as the arms are extensions of the heart.)

7. Imagine that what you are surrounding now is you as a child who had a frightening experience.

   f. Say to the child, "You are safe now. I won't let anyone hurt you." It is safe to say this because this child is holding a moment of your past. They are just a frozen memory that you have come to heal and liberate with Love and Attention. No one but you has your clear access to this moment.

8. Offer the child a hug. This offering helps the child welcome something greater and more powerful than them into their life.

An Integration

Come, let's pray together. Sure, there are many things we may desire; but, let's immerse ourselves in that one great desire of our Soul.

Rumi said it so succinctly when he wrote, "A good gauge of spiritual health is to write down the three things you most want. If they in any way differ, you are in trouble." So let's find that one great want. And let's say to God or Great Mind, "I want You."

These are the words of a prayer. And, what we might feel after uttering these words is the essence of Prayer.

In Essence

Prayer is our attempt to communicate with something or Someone greater than ourselves.

We may pray for something.

Our prayers may be to praise or to give thanks.

But whatever the purpose of our prayer, if there is feeling involved, the outcome will be an exploration of a greater Self.

Chapter 8

SPIRITUAL GROWTH

Awakening to an Already Existing Perfection

All living things grow. Growth and life are inextricably entwined. Human beings, in this life, appear to have a choice in how they wish to grow and what directions they choose. For humans, many realize the pinnacle of growth spiritually. Our souls, already an expression of the Divine, are a still, soft voice urging us to awaken, come home and remember who we truly are and have always been - the Self

Two Stages of Spiritual Growth

Our Spiritual Growth Has Two Stages. They are as follows:

Stage 1 includes the development and maturation of our egos.

Stage 2 is discovering and living from a spiritual identity beyond our egos.

While both stages involve understanding who we are, it is in Stage 2 that this growth appears more directed to our relationship with something greater and more expanded than we are. This could be called Buddha Mind, the Void, Spirit or God, or, The Wisdom of the Group.

It is my belief, and direct experience that multiple lifetimes are a central feature of human growth. I offer to you that we live in a classroom: Classroom Earth. We come into this classroom time after time to learn and grow and to mature. Life after life, we make mistakes and have the opportunity to learn from those mistakes.

In past lives, we have stolen, cheated, harmed, killed, betrayed, and, due to the Law of Cause and Effect and the Law of Karma, these behaviors have returned to us. Each time we have a choice to either keep making the same mistake, or decide we don't want to do this to anyone else, and we don't want it done to us. If we choose growth, we get to move on to the next learning opportunity. Perhaps this next life is about becoming more trustworthy.

Stage 1 is the process of learning to respect the needs and desires of others. It is also about discovering our own real needs. Until the ego has lost its substantial control over our lives and decision-making, it is very difficult to grow spiritually.

Self-Inquiry Questions

- Can you imagine or experience a Higher Self beyond the ego?
- How attached and identified with the ego do you feel?
- Are you making your choices, or are you letting the past and your unconscious choose for you?
- How does Love support spiritual growth?

Stage 1: Maturing Up the Ego: Support, Insight and Suggestions

As you read each quote, you may want to ask yourself: what can I learn from this piece of wisdom, and take time to ask; how can this truth help me to grow?

For example, with Jung's first quote, you may ask yourself: what am I doing to grow more mature? And, what am I doing to let go of my ego?

In the second quote, perhaps you'll ask yourself: What am I doing to inquire within, and how could I do this more effectively?

Quotes About a Healthy Ego

"The first half of life is devoted to forming a healthy ego, the second half is going inward and letting go of it."

~Carl Jung

"But the more we become conscious of ourselves through self-knowledge and act accordingly, the more the layer of the personal unconscious will be diminished. In this way, there arises a consciousness no longer imprisoned in the petty, oversensitive, personal world of the ego, but participates freely in the wider world of objective interests."

~Carl Jung

"Among all my patients in the second half of life…there has not been one whose problem in the last resort was not that of finding a religious outlook on life. It is safe to say that every one of them fell ill because he had lost what the living religions of every age have given their followers, and none of them has really healed who did not regain his religious outlook. This, of course, has nothing to do with a particular creed or membership in a church."

~Carl Jung

"Applicants for wisdom do what I have done: Inquire within."

~Heraclitus

"The spiritual life is more about subtraction than addition."

~Meister Eckhart

"Do you not see how necessary a world of pain and troubles is to school an intelligence and make it a Soul?"

~John Keats

"If someone is a problem for you, it's you who needs to change."

~Ram Dass

"At any moment, you have a choice, that either leads you closer to your spirit or further away from it."

~Thich Nhat Hanh

"To realize that you are not your thoughts is when you begin to awaken spiritually."

~Eckhart Tolle

"Whatever you think the world is withholding from you, you are withholding from the world."

~Eckhart Tolle

"Awakening is not changing who you are, but discarding who you are not."

~Deepak Chopra

"When fundamental acceptance of what is showing up in your life is not enough...sometimes an even more careful and directed attention is needed to open our repeated patterns and deepest knots...knots of energy that have bodily contraction, emotions, memories and images intertwined."

~Jack Kornfield

Stage 2: Growing Spiritually

A Process: Getting Honest

A key to maturing up and moving beyond the ego is to be honest with yourself. What is it that you really want? Do you Love yourself and others? Are you willing to be present with all your feelings? Does your ego crave attention and praise?

You will also slow down your growth if you try to fool yourself, or others, into believing that you just want transformation and enlightenment. Honesty with yourself is food for the soul.

Fill in the following sentence many times. Try to let different answers pour out of you. Don't try to look good. Write down your responses.

If I were candid, and it would be okay to want anything, what I want most is _____.

Now, sit with your answers and explore how you would feel if you got each item on the list.

I believe God isn't saying to come home immediately. I believe God is saying to come home when you're ready, and wherever you find yourself, and what you desire now is the perfect starting place.

But be prepared for the possibility that after you get something that you think you want, it may lead you to a feeling of emptiness.

If I had all the money I could ever want, over time I might feel _____.

If I had all the sex I could ever want, over time I might feel_____.

If I had all the power to make people do what I want, after a number of years I might feel____?

If I could have anything I want to eat at any time, after a number of years I might feel_____?

Do you get a feeling that the pleasures of the senses, and the attempt to fulfill the ego is a world of diminishing returns?

Stage 2 includes learning to be and act from the moment, rather than acting from retained emotions of the past. It is a time for discovering the world that lives within us.

Spiritual growth that leads to the awakening to our Higher and Divine Self is the ultimate objective of our classroom-earth experience.

Spiritual growth involves connection. The more we are connected to the Divine, to Source, to God, the more we grow spiritually. This growth blossoms until our relationship is 100% responsible for our behavior and sense of identity and until we live the phrase: "I am That" or until our identity lies with our Higher or God-Self. Spiritual growth is also about transformation - the transformation of our identity.

In Stage 1, we are identified with our emotions. We might easily say, "I am angry", and feel that our identity as an angry person is who we are at times. We can also identify with our job, our car, our race or our country.

In Stage 2, this limiting identity starts to dissolve, and our sense of who we are grows until enlightenment when we no longer identify ourselves with our egos but with our Divine Nature.

Aspects Of Stage 2: Growth

- Opening the Heart
- Spiritual Practice
- The Role of the Present Moment
- Identifying With Our Higher Self

Opening the Heart

The Indian philosophy of Vedanta holds that there are different paths to union and spiritual awakening. These include the path of the heart (Bhakti yoga), the path of the mind (Jnana yoga), the path of action (Karma yoga) and the path of meditation (Raja yoga). All four paths intertwine and end at the same place. However, Swami Sivananda expressed a perspective shared by many spiritual teachers when he said, Bhakti Yoga is "The easiest, surest and quickest means of God-realization."

But, perhaps the sweetest expression regarding the role of the heart is from Antione Saint-Exupery, "It is only with the heart that one can see rightly; what is essential is invisible to the eye."

If we believe that God is Love, then how could Love not be a path to God? Sufism, in mystical Islam, refers to God as the Beloved, emphasizing the central feature of Love is coming to Allah.

As Rumi, the most famous of the Sufi mystical poets writes, "Love is the cure, for your pain will keep giving birth to more pain until your eyes constantly exhale love as effortlessly as your body yields its scent."

"The Way is not in the sky. The Way is in the heart."

~The Pali Tripitaka

"Big-heartedness is the most essential virtue on the spiritual journey."

~Matthew Fox

"When you plant a seed of love, it is you that blossoms."

~Ma Jaya Sati Bhagavati

"A state of mind that sees God in everything is evidence of growth in grace and a thankful heart."

~Charles Finney

"[The evolved person] considers all people to be his friends and none his foes. In fact, he believes that all those who bring him pain and do him harm are his full and special friends. He is therefore inclined to will them as much good as to the closest friend he has."

~The Cloud of Unknowing

Compassion is the joy of sharing. It's doing small things for the love of each other-just a smile, or carrying a bucket of water, or showing some simple kindness. These are the small things that make up compassion.

~Mother Teresa

"In the final analysis it is between you and God, it was never between you and them anyway."

~Mother Teresa

"Being in love rather than giving or taking love, is the only thing that provides stability."

~Ram Dass

"In undertaking a spiritual life, what matters is simple: We must make certain that our path is connected with our heart. In the end, spiritual life is not a process of seeking or gaining some extraordinary condition or special powers."

~Jack Kornfield

Try it as many times as you think necessary. Then ask yourself alone, one question . . . Does this path have a heart? If it does, the path is good; if it doesn't it is of no use.

~Carlos Castaneda

Spiritual Practice

As one matures deeper into Stage 2, spiritual practice isn't just something one does for 20 minutes twice a day and maybe more on Sunday. More and more, everything we do becomes a form of spiritual practice. For example, if we become upset, our practice will examine where this upset is coming from and bring healing and consciousness to the re-trained emotion within us.

Quotes About Becoming Conscious

Practice is every person you meet; practice is every unkind word you hear or that may even be directed at you."

~Sogyal Rinpoche

"As we follow a genuine path of practice, our sufferings may seem to increase because we no longer hide from them or from ourselves."

~Jack Kornfield

"Eventually, all that one has learnt will have to be forgotten."

~Ramana Maharshi

Let come what comes, let go what goes. Find out what remains."

~Ramana Maharshi

"And the day came when the risk to remain tight in a bud was more painful than the risk it took to blossom."

~Anais Nin

"The key to spiritual maturation is transforming all of life, adversity included, into spiritual practice."

~B. Alan Wallace

"…nothing ever goes away until it has taught us what we need to know."

~Pema Chödrön

"Each of you is perfect the way you are ... and you can use a little improvement."

~Shunryu Suzuki

"When you are spiritually connected, you are not looking for occasions to be offended, and you are not judging and labeling others. You are in a state of grace in which you know you are connected to God and thus free from the effects of anyone or anything external to yourself."

~Wayne Dyer

"Imagine that every person in the world is enlightened but you. They are all your teachers, each doing just the right things to help you learn perfect patience, perfect wisdom, perfect compassion."

~Buddha

"Spiritual practice is not just sitting meditation. Practice is looking, touching, drinking, eating and talking. Every act, every breath, and every step can be practice and can help us to become more ourselves."

~Thich Nhat Hanh

"I feel that the essence of spiritual practice is your attitude towards others. When you have a pure, sincere motivation, then you have right attitude toward others based on kindness, compassion, Love and respect."

~H.H. The Dalai Lama

"The source of your mind is love and whatever you do to go to that source is a spiritual practice."

~Sri Sri Ravi Shankar

"The goal of spiritual practice is full recovery, and the only thing you need to recover from is a fractured sense of self."

~Marianne Williamson

The Role of the Present Moment

There is nothing real in the past as it is stored in our minds. All of our memories are perceptions, fragments, projections and distortions. The way out of the limitation of memories is to enter the present, the Now. The Now is the point of power. The Now is where the Real is available.

"Every breath we take, every step we take, can be filled with peace, joy and serenity... We need only to be awake, alive in the present moment."

~Thich Nhat Hanh

"The moment is all there is."

~Rumi

"Realize deeply that the present moment is all you have. Make the NOW the primary focus of your life."

~Eckhart Tolle

"It is through gratitude for the present moment that the spiritual dimension of life opens up."

~Eckhart Tolle

"You must live in the present, launch yourself on every wave, find your eternity in each moment."

~Henry David Thoreau

"The new day is too dear, with its hopes and invitations, to waste a moment on the yesterdays."

~Ralph Waldo Emerson

Quotes About Identifying With the Higher Self

"Within you, there is a stillness and a sanctuary to which you can retreat at any time and be yourself."

~Hermann Hesse

"The experience of being separate arises out of a shell of protection that is formed to numb the feeling of very young pain. This shell doesn't just numb the pain, it also numbs the feeling of connection with everything."

~Devaji

"The truth is, everything will be okay as soon as you are okay with everything. And that's the only time everything will be okay."

~Michael A. Singer

"Rather than being your thoughts and emotions, be the awareness behind them."

~Eckhart Tolle

"What if nothing is wrong?"

~Adyashanti

"The maturing process is a journey to independence. Our spiritual journeys are just the opposite. We start off in rebellion against God, thinking we are fully independent from Him.

Spiritual maturity, then, is the process of recognizing our complete dependence on God and learning to rely on Him and not ourselves."

~Christian perspective

"All great spirituality teaches about letting go of what you don't need and who you are not."

~Richard Rohr

"The privilege of a lifetime is to become who you really are."

~Carl Jung

A Passageway Visualization to the Present Moment

Imagine if you will, that you are standing in a hallway. There are three doors to your right and three doors to your left. There is a single door at the end of the hallway, and you are facing this door. The doors to your right and the doors to your left lead to memories. These are memories stored in your mind, memories that live in the past. The single door facing you leads to the Present Moment.

1. Walk down the hallway with the intent to stay present, not to open the six doors of memories. When you open the door you are facing, you will be led to a beautiful, safe, and fulfilling scene of nature created just for you at this moment.

2. Open the door and step out, and use your senses to appreciate the beauty before you.

   a. Feel the softness of the green grass and smell the wildflowers.

   b. Hear the breeze rustling through the trees.

   c. Your senses connect you to the Present Moment.

3. Most importantly, feel the sunshine on your body.

   d. Notice that the sun is giving warmth, healing, life-sustaining energy, and it is giving everything to you with no demand or expectation. It doesn't care what you have done or will do; it is an unconditional give. It is a perfect metaphor for unconditional Love (for God's Love if that term works for you).

4. Just let yourself be loved for no reason.

5. Now, just be silent. You may notice that your mind is quiet.

   e. You may sense your ego-self is diminished or reduced; or, perhaps it is even eliminated for a moment.

Welcome to the Present Moment!

Help Along the Spiritual Path

- Sangha

- Selfless Service/Seva

- Satsang

- Teacher/Guru/Guide
- Spiritual Community

Sangha

Sangha is a Sanskrit word meaning community. When used in a spiritual context, it is a group of people who support each other through spiritual practice. Many believe that such a community is spiritually essential.

"And what we can do is we can

Help each other along.

We can be the satsang, the sangha, the spiritual community,

The support for one another.

Giving each other the confidence to keep pursuing this possibility."

~Ram Dass citing Hesse

"In Buddhism, there are three gems: Buddha, the awakened one; Dharma, the way of understanding and loving; and Sangha, the community that lives in harmony and awareness... A good community is needed to help us resist the unwholesome ways of our time...With the support of friends in the practice, peace has a chance."

~Thich Nhat Hanh

"The jewel of community, the Sangha, is to be held equal to the Buddha and the Dharma. Indeed, the whole of holy life is fulfilled through spiritual friendship."

~Buddha

Selfless Service/Seva

Selfless service is an action that we perform without any expectation of personal reward.

Many spiritual communities use the Sanskrit word Seva to highlight the spiritual benefits of acting without self-interest. By going beyond our self in action, we prepare ourselves to go beyond ourselves in consciousness.

"Only a life lived for others is a life worth living."

~Albert Einstein

"We make a living by what we get, but we make a life by what we give."

~Winston Churchill

"The best way to find yourself is to lose yourself in the service of others."

~Mahatma Gandhi

"Everybody can be great…because anybody can serve."

~Martin Luther King Jr.

"I slept and dreamt that life was joy. I awoke and saw that life was service. I acted and behold, service was joy."

~Rabindranath Tagore

"Your own Self-Realization is the greatest service you can render the world."

~Ramana Maharshi

"All acts of service are meaningless unless they are given with love."

~Sai Baba

"The deepest form of seva…is to forgo the conditioned mind's desire to get, and just to remain, which is remaining still."

~Devaji

"The highest truth cannot be put into words. Therefore the greatest teacher has nothing to say. He simply gives himself in service, and never worries."

~Lao Tzu

Satsang

Satsang is also a Sanskrit word meaning to come together to inquire into our True Nature. It also can refer to devotional singing or a spiritual discourse given by an enlightened teacher.

"Satsang is here to wash off the minds face and to reveal the face of God."

~Mooji

"The psychological mind, in Satsang, is like a piece of ice placed in a bowl of warm water."

~Mooji

"Satsang means two things:

1. Intellectual discussion, which is totally a left-brain activity

2. Singing, which is a right-brain activity. Both are necessary."

~Sri Sri Ravi Shankar

"It should be for satsang that we go to spiritual centers…Even though the breeze blows everywhere, coolness will be felt more if we sit in the shade of a tree. In the same way, although God is all-pervading, this presence will clearly shine in certain places more than others."

~Mata Amritanandamayi

Teacher/Guru/Guide

Many spiritual traditions believe that one must have an awakened teacher to awaken in this life. Other spiritual traditions place no focus on enlightenment. However, almost all spiritual traditions acknowledge the importance of a teacher.

"The guru must be one who has known, has actually realized the Divine truth, has perceived himself as the spirit…The one who has the power of transmitting this current is called a Guru."

~Swami Vivekananda

"I am the way, the truth, and the life. No one comes to the Father except through Me."

~Jesus *(John: 14:6, King James Version)*

"I have never said that there is no need for a guru. All depends on what you call guru. He need not be in a human form." ~Ramana Maharshi

"Let no man in the world live in delusion. Without a Guru none can cross over to the other shore."

~Gurū Nānak

"The Guru cannot awaken you; all that he can do is to point out what is."

~Jiddu Krishnamurti

"You have to be your own teacher."

~Jiddu Krishnamurti

"There is no guru like our own mistakes."

~Ilaiyaraaja

"The true tzaddik connects you to your G-d without ever standing in the way."

~Menachem Mendel Schneerson

A tzaddik, says Rebbe Schneerson is one whose self is Love, awe and faith and for whom there is no death.

"If your teacher is enlightened or in a lineage of enlightened teachers, that state will be more tangible for you than if your teacher is in the second generation..."

~Sally Kempton

"Isn't it interesting that guru is spelled g (gee) u (you) r (are) u (you)?

~Humorist Steve Bhaerman *(aka Swami Beyondananda)*

"A Guru is a friend who constantly tramples your ego. It's a very delicate operation."

~Sadhguru

"Don't go searching for a Guru. When the pain of ignorance within you becomes a scream, a Guru will come in search of you."

~Sadhguru

"The Guru is the conveyance which the spiritual influence is brought to you. Anyone can teach, but the spirit must be passed on by the Guru to the Shishya (disciple), and that will fructify."

~Swami Vivekananda

A Process: Making Ourselves Ready To Be Taught

There is a saying: teaching waits on welcome, not need. To be taught, we need to make ourselves available and open.

There is a teaching story: A professor goes to meet and learn from the Zen master. The professor tells the Master all he has studied, and learned, and how advanced he is and ready to be with the Zen teacher. The Master is pouring tea for the professor, and he keeps pouring, even though the cup is overflowing. The professor says, "What are you doing? The cup is too full. There is no room in it for any more." "Exactly the situation here with you," replies the Master.

Zen calls this openness "beginner's mind". One Zen Master's approach to learning is "only don't know."

Jesus said, "I tell you the truth, unless you change and become like the little children, you will never enter the kingdom of heaven." *(Matthew 18:3 - New International Version)*

A Visualization

1. Imagine that you are sitting on the ground in a circle of students who have come to learn from a great enlightened master.

2. Imagine that the Master (either male or female) is one of the wisest, most radiant beings you have ever met. Their Presence stops your mind in its tracks. You feel nothing but Peace.

   a. The Master says, "Nothing that your mind holds now will awaken you. Nothing that you have ever done or not done will hold you back in this moment. Do not compare this moment to anything from the past."

3. "Now slip," the Master continues, "into the radiant Light of this moment. Do not hold on to your little sense of self-identity.

   b. Just be with me in the Light. This is Innocence. This is the doorway to Reality."

An Integration

We live in an expanding universe, and while it is expanding, life is expanding and evolving. Our lives are expanding as well. Lifetime after lifetime, we grow more spiritually mature. We learn through our mistakes. And then, the time comes when we have broken free of the chrysalis, of the ego and taken flight into freedom. We have made the journey and awakened into our Self.

Perhaps we had many teachers like Buddha, but awoke on our own. Maybe we were aided by a lineage of masters. Possibly our awakening was spontaneous, even unimagined.

Far and wide, the enlightened Masters assure us. They say that everything born of God returns to God. Love will never experience Itself as separate from anything.

Until that completion, our job is to yearn for our Wholeness, yearn for our place in God's embrace. And then life allows us to make our yearning real through action that leads us in the direction we espouse, the direction Home.

In Essence

There comes a time when gratifying our egos is simply not enough.

Perhaps it comes in this life, perhaps in another. But, when it does come, spiritual growth is the only solution for the uneasiness, boredom and flatness of life lived through the ego.

When this stage arrives, help comes, people appear, even angels show up.

There is no right path. For everyone's journey is different.

And, many paths seem to end, and new ones begin. But, there is an underlying feeling of excitement, a feeling of being led.

We are going Home.

Chapter 9

ENLIGHTENMENT

Living From the Authentic Self

E nlightened masters tell us that we are already enlightened. By this, they mean that we are not our egoic, self-created identity. We are not who our ego tells us we are. We are, in our true nature, already unbounded, already eternal.

The masters tell us that enlightenment is just a shift of identity. One moment I identify as Rick and then, in enlightenment, I identify as unbounded awareness and observe that I have an identity as Rick. A shifting of self-awareness from the right foot to the left, if you will.

The spiritual journey, described by many names, has always been, in essence, to slip the invisible bonds and confinement of our self-created egoic identity. This growth allows us to live in the freedom, peace, and awareness of the already existing eternal Self within.

In God-based, mystical traditions, the state of enlightenment reveals our Divine Nature and oneness with God. In the Hindu religion, one awakens to the Self as Brahma, the Creator of all.

In mystical Christianity, the egoic self disappears to permit the Father within to act through us. Saint Teresa of Avila described the enlightened experience this way: "I have no seams, no walls, no laws. My frontiers and God's are the same."

The kabbalist of mystical Judaism yearns to recover the cosmic consciousness of Adam and Eve before the fruit of knowledge was tasted. They seek this consciousness without renouncing the world. In the Sufi experience of mystical Islam, enlightenment is union with the Beloved.

From the Buddhist perspective, enlightenment refers to being awakened to our True Nature. From this awakened state, one can further attain supreme Buddhahood, as exemplified by Gautama Buddha.

Enlightenment has long been held as the Spiritual-Summit of human endeavor. However, enlightenment is not just one experience.

The Master-Teachers tell us that there are stages in the unfoldment to complete and total permanent enlightenment. While for most, these stages unfold sequentially, some report instantaneous enlightenment.

A process will be offered later in the chapter to offer a sense of the early stages of enlightenment.

Self-Inquiry Questions

- How open do you feel to explore an identity that transcends your ego?

- Would you welcome an experience of unboundedness and stillness?

- Does the concept of infinite bliss attract you and do you believe it's possible?

- Do you equate the unbounded with God?

Quotes About the Richness of Enlightenment

"One day He did not leave after kissing me."

~Rabia of Basra *(aka Rabia al-Basri)*

"Immortality is freedom from the feeling: 'I am.' Yet it is not extinction. On the contrary, it is a state infinitely more real, aware and happy than you can possibly think of. Only self-consciousness is no more."

~Sri Nisargadatta Maharaj

"To enjoy good health, to bring true happiness to one's family, to bring peace to all, one must first discipline and control one's own mind. If a man can control his mind he can find the way to Enlightenment, and all wisdom and virtue will naturally come to him."

~Buddha

"Unenlightened existence is inherently unsatisfactory."

~Buddha's First Noble Truth

"Enlightenment for a wave is the moment the wave realizes that it is water. At that moment, all fear of death disappears."

~Thich Nhat Hanh

"To know yourself as the Being underneath the thinker, the stillness underneath the mental noise, the love and joy underneath the pain, is freedom, salvation, enlightenment."

~Eckhart Tolle

"Understand this great truth: the happiness that comes from the pleasures of the world is but a minute reflection of the infinite bliss that comes from within your own Self."

~Amma

The Seven States of Consciousness and Enlightenment

What is the state of enlightenment referred to in all major Spiritual Traditions around the world? Do all of the different names from all of the various traditions refer to the same thing?

Let's begin with a very clarifying and helpful description of what Maharishi Mahesh Yogi calls the seven states of consciousness, and how they relate to Enlightenment.

Maharishi Mahesh Yogi taught that there are seven major states of consciousness that are experientially and scientifically distinct. Experientially, the seven states of consciousness feel and are very different from each other.

From the scientific perspective, if you were fitted with appropriate electrodes and equipment, a researcher in another room could determine your state of consciousness at that moment.

Let's Look at the First Four States of Consciousness:

1. **Waking State:** This is our ordinary everyday reality.

2. **Dreaming State:** this is when we have REM activity, and a story unfolds while in a sleep state.

3. **Deep Sleep State:** In this sleep state, there is no self-awareness, just unconsciousness.

4. **Transcendental State/ Pure Awareness/The Absolute:** During transcendence, one is unaware of a personal self. One becomes immersed in Being or Pure Awareness. Immediately following such an experience, one may be aware of feeling expanded or blissful and

unquestionably, profoundly quiet. During the event, there is little to no mental activity. As a result of ongoing transcendental practice and experience, our lifelong identification with our egoic sense of personal-self becomes weaker and weaker as a sense of an expanded awareness of Inherent-Self grows stronger.

Transcendence and the Growing Absence of the Sense of Personal-Self

Most of us live predominantly in the first three states of consciousness as described by Maharishi: waking, dreaming, and sleeping. Those who live every day in these first three levels of consciousness have a strong sense of who they believe they are. They have a self-constructed self-identity. There is nothing wrong with this. It is essential to the process of awakening.

From the perspective of enlightenment, however, this self-constructed self-identity is an illusion. Masters often refer to this everyday, egoic-consciousness as living in a "dream."

Reaching and experiencing the Enlightened state is a very individual process. At first, it's temporary and fleeting. It generally requires practice. Because of the individual nature of reaching an enlightenment state of consciousness, one may need a wide variety of learning experiences and even a wide variety of teachers and helpers along the way to awaken from the 'dream' successfully.

Think of it like a bucket brigade used to put out a fire. In this bucket brigade, many people, many helpers, line up to aid the joint effort. Each person passes a bucket of water to the next person in the line. The last person in line throws the last bucket of water on the fire and finally extinguishes it.

In this metaphor, the fire represents the burning insistence and persistence of our self-created egos. A lovely aspect of this story is that everyone in the bucket brigade is of utmost importance, not just the last one putting the fire out.

Quotes About the Growing Sense of Enlightenment

"All at once, as it were out of the intensity of the consciousness of individuality, individuality itself seemed to dissolve and fade away into boundless being, and this not a confused state but the clearest of the clear, the surest of the sure, utterly beyond words – where death was an almost laughable impossibility – the loss of personality (if it were so) seemingly no extinction but the only true life."

~Alfred Lord Tennyson

"Desires still flow into the mind of the seer, but he is no longer disturbed by them."

~Bhagavad Gita

"Like a little stream

Making its way

Through the mossy crevices

I, too, quietly

Turn clear and transparent."

~Ryokan

"Everybody wants to get enlightened but nobody wants to change."

~Andrew Cohen

"There are many paths to enlightenment. Be sure to take the one with a heart."

~Lao Tzu

"At last nothing remained but a pure, absolute, abstract Self. The universe became without form and void of content. But Self persisted, formidable in its vivid keenness…"

~J.A. Symonds

"The land of nothing whatsoever is our real home."

~Chuang Tzu

"Attain utmost emptiness. Abide in steadfast stillness."

~Lao Tzu

"Enlightenment is but a recognition, not a change at all."

~A Course in Miracles

"The true value of a human being can be found in the degree to which he has attained liberation from the self."

~Albert Einstein

"One does not become enlightened by imagining figures of light, but by making the darkness conscious."

~Carl Jung

"If you think you're enlightened, try going home for the weekend."

~ Ram Dass

Let's Look at the Next Three States of Consciousness As Described by Maharishi Mahesh Yogi.

1. **Cosmic Consciousness:** In this, the transcendental state of Pure Consciousness is maintained along with waking activity. One is now identified with their more expanded sense of awareness rather than with their limited individual, egoic nature.

Bring to mind the idea of having two legs, an egoic leg, and a cosmic-conscious leg. Imagine that you are standing on both legs. In the state of cosmic consciousness, the cosmic leg, which is the more dominant leg, would be the one holding your weight. We can choose to focus on the egoic leg but we identify with the cosmically-conscious leg.

One might say, "I have legs, but I am not my legs. I have an ego, but I am not an ego."

Another way of understanding this state is called "Witnessing". One witnesses the activity much like watching a play or movie but is not the actor. Witnessing is a very interesting phenomenon and a powerful spiritual tool.

While we maintain an awareness of our transcendental nature, we are also aware of our egoic consciousness. For example, we may witness our ego feeling jealous or angry, but not identify with these feelings. We are just observing how our ego is feeling at that moment. While Witnessing, we are aware of two experiences of consciousness, but only identified with our expanded state.

2. **Refined Cosmic Consciousness or God Consciousness:** In this, the nervous system has become further refined and is able to perceive Divine Presence on the surface of everything. As Maharishi describes it: Qualities of the Absolute, which in cosmic consciousness were limited to the subjective level, begin to overflow into the world at large. Thus the world, as well as the Self, is seen to be filled with the divine.

3. **Unity Consciousness:** In this state, all is experienced as One. Maharishi says that after Refined Cosmic Consciousness has been stabilized for some time, perception becomes still subtler, to include not only the finest relative worldly aspects but also the omnipresent Absolute. Everything is God. Everything is the One.

Quotes About Cosmic Consciousness

"Spiritual realization is to see clearly that what I perceive, experience, think, or feel is ultimately not who I am, that I cannot find myself in all those things that continually pass away.

~Eckhart Tolle

"The state we call Realization is simply being one's self, not knowing anything or becoming anything...the Real is ever present...All that is required to realize the Self is to be Still." ~Ramana Maharshi

"There is only the notion of self to be transcended."

~Thich Nhat Hanh

"Enlightenment is the inner light of wisdom that is permanently free from all mistaken appearance, and whose function is to bestow mental peace upon each and every living being every day."

~Kelsang Gyatso

"Enlightenment is a shift in self-identification from body to spirit."

~A Course in Miracles

"My Guru, before he died, told me: 'Believe me, you are the Supreme Reality. Don't doubt my words, don't disbelieve me. I am telling you the truth, act on it. I could not forget his words and by not forgetting, I have realized.'"

~Sri Nisargadatta Maharaj

Quotes About Refined Cosmic Consciousness

"One sees God absolutely everywhere when one loves with Divine Love."

~Ramakrishna

"The tzaddik doesn't see a world. He only sees and hears G-d teaching him."

~Tzvi Freeman summarizing a statement of Rebbe Menachem Schneerson.

A tzaddik, in Chassidic thought, is one who has conquered his animal soul.

Master and monk are walking upon the mountain path and the master asks, "Do you smell the mountain laurel?"

The monk responds, "Yes."

To which the master replies, "There, I have held nothing back from you."

~Daisetz Teitaro Suzuki

"Loving you, I enlightened myself."

~Sw. Chidananda Tirtha

Quotes About Unity

"Enlightenment is intimacy with all things."

~Dogen Zenji

"As the Union grows more complete, the link of worship, of adoration and devotion, finds fulfillment in its own extinction, leaving worshippers together in perfect oneness, in the oneness of absolute Unity."

~Maharishi Mahesh Yogi

"I swam in the ocean of divinity until I went beyond the Trinity."

~Meister Eckhart.

"My being is God, not by simple participation but by true transformation. My I is God; there is no other I."

~St. Catherine of Genoa

"We shall be in such oneness with the Source of All Life until there shall be nothing to distinguish between the created being and the Creator."

~Rabbi Menachem Mendel Schneerson

"When all things are nothing but God, there are then no things and no God, but only this. No objects, no subjects, only this."

~Ken Wilber

"When we try to pick out anything by itself, we find it hitched to everything else in the universe."

~John Muir

"Thou art That."

~ Chandogya Upanishad

This famous great saying in its original Sanskrit is, "Tat Tvam Asi" (That art Thou), the expression of the relationship between the individual and the Absolute. This insight can also be used to describe the 5th, 6th and 7th states of consciousness when expanded to: I am That. Thou art That. All this is nothing but That.

"The birds have vanished down the sky,

and now the last cloud drains away.

We sit together, the mountain and me,

until only the mountain remains."

~Li Bai (aka Li Po)

Many Names

There seem to be many names relating to the 4th, 5th, 6th, and 7th state of consciousness:

Self Realization can refer to any experience of 4-7.

Satori is a Buddhist term for a sudden, inexpressible feeling of inner understanding or enlightenment. "Satori is to be with God before the universe was created," wrote D.T. Suzuki.

Nirvana is a Buddhist term for an inner state of bliss.

Awakened is a term that refers to a permanent experience of states 5-7.

Freedom is used as a state of non-attachment to anything while experiencing the unboundedness of Being or Pure Consciousness.

Moksa *(also called Mukti)* is the Hindu or Sanskrit term for the final release of the soul or consciousness from Samsara (the wheel of birth and death,) and the bringing to an end of all suffering involved in being subject to the cycle of repeated death and rebirth.

Samadhi is a Sanskrit term for immersion in Pure Consciousness or transcendental awareness.

Revealing the Enlightenment Within

The Masters teach us that enlightenment is our natural state. They write, "We are already enlightened".

So, to live from this internal enlightened state is to free ourselves from the egoic covering, the illusion of limitation.

The advice they give includes: meditation to purify the nervous system, choosing stillness, freeing ourselves from the habit of distraction, giving attention to what we have hidden in our unconscious, service to others, acceptance of what is right now, devotion, prayer, and wanting to rid the illusion more than anything else.

An Experiential Exercise

Repeating an image used before, imagine that you are standing on both feet.

1. Now, put your weight and full attention on your right foot.

    a. We'll call this posture being in the ego.

    b. The other foot is still there, but pay no attention to it.

2. Now, place your weight evenly between both legs.

    c. We'll say this state is reflective of a growing awareness of our Higher Self, our nature as Being. We are aware that both states exist within us.

3. Now, finally, place all your attention on your left leg.

4. Using a Zen Koan as a helper, ask yourself, "What did my face look like before I was born?"

    d. Allow there to be no way your mind can answer the question and allow it to just be still.

5. Now, allow there to be a possibility of your consciousness spreading out.

    e. This sense of expansion and stillness may give you a taste of identifying with expansion and Being rather than just a right leg egoic personality.

An Integration

Imagine that more than anything, you want to live in the freedom, peace, and the joy of liberation from identification with your ego.

Imagine that your desire is so focused that "thine eye be single" and therefore your body is filled with Light. And, imagine again that you look at everything with the eyes of Love. And, therefore see rightly.

These experiences and more wait for us in the enlightened state.

The Master-Teachers tell us that this is not some far-off dream. They tell us that enlightenment already lives fully within us, like an ever-present sun.

Our job is to remove the clouds that obscure this brilliance. We are like a family of trees. And we know that if one tree in a family can flower then all trees in that family can flower.

Enlightenment is the full flowering of the human being.

In Essence

"Thou art That."

Our inherent nature is unbounded.

Our ego is a vehicle for our growth and awakening.

Our lives will find ultimate fulfillment upon awakening to our eternal and bliss-infused nature.

This is enlightenment.

This is Reality.

Chapter 10

RELATIONSHIPS

Four Approaches To Help Relationships Thrive

A ll relationships have the potential to be a huge source of joy or an enormous cause of sorrow. They can offer one of life's most profound healing opportunities, or they can bring out the worst in us. As novelist Anne Lamott is quoted as saying, "Getting into a new relationship is like pouring Miracle-Gro (™) on your character defects.".

Most relationships are a combination of joy, suffering and growth potential. When we recognize the importance of relationships, it is troubling and sad to realize that relationships may be where we may have the least training and the most baggage.

All successful relationships have the same starting place: Self-respect and Self-Love. If we can't accept and Love ourselves, we can't Love anyone else either. When Self-Love is present, relationships can be the most glorious part of being human. Love may be for a person, an animal, nature or God. It doesn't matter. When it is Great-Love, its source is the Divine. It reveals the best of us.

Our ego-based relationships with others are a projected expression of our thoughts, feelings, judgments, and ultimately the degree to which we have come to Love ourselves. We project our experiences onto others; and, our most potent, and lasting projections come from our relationships with our mothers, fathers, or other caregivers. Projection is especially damaging in our romantic relationships.

Unconsciously, most people enter into romantic relationships with self-centered and unrealistic expectations. Unknowingly, many people are repeating failed patterns learned from their parents with potentially disastrous results. Even worse, our egoic behavior can turn a promising opportunity for Love into an emotional train wreck.

We express and manifest our spiritual growth in our relationship with the Divine; or, described from the Buddhist perspective, the Ground of Being. For this relationship to reach its potential, it must grow out of Love. To be in a relationship with God or Being out of fear, will always be limited. It will be a relationship with a contracted ego that does not know the Infinite.

The lessons in this chapter were learned by experiencing and maturing through a variety of challenging relationships. My hard work has resulted in the wonderful relationship and marriage that I now have with Robin and have dreamed of for my whole adult life.

How Can We Expand and Improve Our Relationships?

There are thousands of books written on relationships of all kinds. Such an in-depth study is beyond the scope of a single chapter. Still, I can offer four approaches that can help make all relationships more successful. I distilled the following from over 30-years in a professional healing practice. More importantly, these guidelines are the bedrock for the deeply-loving marriage I share with my wife.

Four Approaches To Help Relationships Thrive

1. **Grow:** View all relationships as an opportunity for egoic maturation. Start and finish with Self-Love.

2. **Accept and Embrace Your Feelings:** Envision the relationship as a call to emotional healing. Emotional maturity is essential for relationships with depth.

3. **Find Real Love:** In romantic relationships, accept romance as a great beginning, intimacy as the next step, Great Love as the basis for being and having a Soul Partner.

4. **See the Good and the God in the Other:** Think of all relationships as an opportunity for spiritual growth and connection with the One.

Self-Inquiry Questions

- Can you regard your limitations as opportunities to Love yourself unconditionally, rather than judge yourself?

- How often do you blame others when you get angry, disappointed or frustrated?

- Are you open to discovering more profound Love if the romantic aspect of your relationship fades?

- Is it possible that God Loves you exactly as you are?

1: Ego Maturation: Challenges to Growth

Our chronological age is not always a good indicator of our egoic maturity. Ego maturity is the result of attention, work and motivation. Sometimes that motivation comes from within.

More often than not, it is encouraged or even demanded by others close to you. A mature ego demonstrates the following qualities:

- Self-respect and self-acceptance
- Respect for others and their boundaries
- Emotional balance
- Responsibility
- Self-control
- Ability to plan for and realize goals
- Ability to learn
- Motivated by interests, not fear

When we are not conscious, we are unaware of our inner state. All the unresolved traumas, disappointments, and repressed emotions live in the unconscious, estimated to be approximately 95 % of our minds. To grow in any significant way, the unconscious requires attention and healing.

There Are Essentially Three Stages in Which Problems Can Occur for Egoic Maturation. They Are:

1. **Childhood years** are a time of rapid growth. They are also a time of impulsivity, neediness, and narcissism. Children are vulnerable and often abused, unloved and neglected. Children may also be over-protected and smothered. Unless they are

given the needed attention, childhood issues remain in the unconscious, regardless of our age, and often for life. Typical childhood unconscious patterns might include: No one loves me; I have to please to be loved; It's not fair; It's not safe to be me; You can't make me; My feelings are unimportant, and I can't make it on my own.

2. **Teenage years** are governed by hormones, desire, a need to differentiate, grow and prove our worth to ourselves and others. Teenage issues remain in our unconscious, regardless of our age, and unless given attention, they too, cause problems for life. Typical teenage limiting beliefs and patterns might include: I won't do it your way; Adults are against me; Anger protects me; What my friends think is the truth, and life sucks.

3. **Adult years** are ideally, a time to develop and use our learned abilities successfully. Adult years are a time to establish a philosophy of life, live with integrity, be of service and grow into our Best selves. Unfortunately, many adults have not moved beyond the issues of childhood and teenage years. If this is the case, although such individuals are of adult age, they are not open to input, emotional growth, or correction. Typical adult limiting beliefs might include: I'm an adult, and therefore I know better; To correct or teach me makes me feel like a child; Power over others is how I get even; I'm an adult – you can't tell me what to do, and If I'm not right I will feel ashamed.

Quotes About Growth and Egoic Maturation

" ...the understanding that what we are experiencing in relationship is a reflection of our own internal state of being."

~Jett Psaris and Marlena S Lyons

"You can make more friends in two months by becoming interested in other people than you can in two years by trying to get other people interested in you."

~Dale Carnegie

"Complaining is one of the ego's favorite strategies for strengthening itself."

~Eckhart Tolle

"The moment you become aware of the ego in you, it is strictly no longer the ego but just an old, conditioned mind pattern. Ego implies unawareness. Awareness and ego cannot coexist."

~Eckhart Tolle

"More the knowledge, lesser the Ego. Lesser the knowledge, more the Ego."

~Albert Einstein

"The goal is not to be better than the other man, but your previous self."

- H.H. Dalai Lama

2: Accept and Embrace Your Feelings: Emotional Healing

Years ago, emotions like anger, resentment, jealousy, shame, and fear were rarely encouraged, or even permitted in children. Most likely, they were frowned upon or punished. Societal pressure taught young males to be tough and hide their emotions. Young females were also pressured to disown their feelings. They were taught to be sweet, accommodating, acceptable, and lovable.

The feelings we were not allowed to show did not just disappear. These feelings were repressed, hidden and disowned; but, they remained in the unconscious, subconscious and the body.

Most of us have unconscious parts of ourselves that were hurt in childhood. In adult life, these hurt parts are like invisible magnets for attracting people who will trigger us. Perhaps we felt unloved, or abused by our parents or caregivers, picked on by our siblings, or treated unfairly by our teachers. To heal, we need to bring our repressed and hidden emotions to consciousness.

Perhaps you had a narcissistic mother who only thought about herself. If so, the hurt may result in a desperate desire to please others to feel a sense of egoic-love. It could lead you to feel so alone and hopeless that you might shut down emotionally and be unable to give or receive Love. Or, it could unconsciously draw you to narcissistic women.

Perhaps you had an angry father, emotionally and physically abusive. Carrying this hurt and rejection might make you explode at the slightest provocation. It could result in an inability to stand up for yourself and your beliefs. Or, it could cause you to be attracted to angry, unavailable men.

The nature of the unconscious is that our wounds from the past are invisible, but their effects are very real.

Without the deep emotional healing needed, our relationships will be constant battlegrounds. Our egos will live a less than optimal life based on our unhealed past. We might equate Love with abuse; and, rarely, if ever, can the Love from another fully heal these wounds.

The good news is that the person who needs to Love and accept us, more than any other, is ourselves. Self-Love will heal these wounds. But, until we have developed the ability to Love ourselves unconditionally, we will remain emotionally fragile, defensive and insecure.

A Process: Emotional Healing

Bring to awareness an emotion that is troubling to you.

1. Imagine that you can be present with that emotion, like a parent with a sick child. You can't make the sickness go away, but your Presence is healing.

2. As you sit with the emotion, put a little smile on your lips. This smile will further activate compassion.

3. If you choose, you can speak comforting words to the emotion.

4. Continue this Process for between two-five minutes.

5. Ask yourself, is this emotion as troubling as it was before?

I believe that what makes this Process effective, is that Presence is a Divine quality, and therefore it heals.

Quotes About Feeling and Emotional Healing

"When dealing with people, remember you are not dealing with creatures of logic, but creatures of emotion."

~Dale Carnegie

"Most of us have unrelenting longings for whatever was missing from our childhood."

~David Richo

"As long as our negative self-image remains unconscious, we think our pain, suffering or dissatisfaction in relationship is a result of our partner's behaviors."

~Jett Psaris and Marlena S Lyons

"We do not change to be accepted; we change because we are accepted."

~Paraphrased from Carl Rogers

"Your relationships are all in how you think about the other people in your life…they may behave in ways that you find offensive. However, your relationship to them when they behave offensively is not determined by their behavior, it is determined only by how you choose to relate to their behavior."

~Wayne Dyer

"No one can make you feel inferior without your consent."

~Eleanor Roosevelt

"And the day came when the risk to remain tight in a bud was more painful than the risk it took to blossom."

~Anais Nin

"If your emotional abilities aren't in hand, if you don't have self-awareness, if you are not able to manage your distressing emotions, if you can't have empathy and have effective relationships, then no matter how smart you are, you are not going to get very far."

~Daniel Goleman

"That's all drugs and alcohol do, they cut off your emotions in the end."

~Ringo Starr

"The emotion that can break your heart is sometimes the very one that heals it."

~Nicholas Sparks

3. Finding Love: Romance, Intimacy, and a Soul Partner

Love does not exist between two egos or two bodies; it exists between two Souls.

Romance is not the reality of Love. However, romance to our egos is perhaps one of the most exciting experiences it will ever know. Romance is usually a period of limited duration. Most often, it lasts between three and nine months.

Romance is a time when our egos believe that our partner will fulfill all our desires and fantasies. It is a period of emotional and brain-chemical intoxication, and many of us try to remain in this phase.

This phase comes to an end when we start to see the faults and limitations in our partners. Partners will need to look beyond their intoxication with their fantasy and begin to see the Soul of the person they Love. If they cannot do this, then their relationship will grow more and more unfulfilling. It will become more conflictual as partners blame each other for their unhappiness.

As relationships evolve between mature partners, intimacy follows. Intimacy is a willingness and ability to be open, authentic and vulnerable. Whether it is with a friend or a loved one, intimacy, understanding, and closeness help a relationship to become deeper and richer.

A play on words reveals its power: intimacy is "into-me-see." When we let others see our emotions, fears, joys, challenges, and our friend or partner reciprocates and supports us, trust, affection and intimacy grow.

Finding Love

Our Soul is Love, a part of the Divine. Our Soul yearns to give and receive care, compassion, kindness, respect and devotion. Our yearnings for Unconditional, Universal, non-judgmental Love are the most profound and compelling of all human emotions and needs.

For some, Love was deeply experienced in the past, and it now guides their lives, and searches for the right partner. Some were fortunate enough to experience the bliss of Unconditional Love in childhood, and then, due to life circumstances, it was gone.

For many of us, there never was Unconditional Love, there was only conditional egoic-love that had to be earned, and could be lost or taken away at any time. Good, bad, or indifferent, all childhood experiences influence our choice of partners in adulthood. Our lives are often a search for what we perceive to be Great-Love.

Repetition Compulsion

Whatever a child has experienced from their parents and caregivers is registered in the unconscious as Love. It doesn't matter whether it was hurtful or neglectful, abusive, or unreliable, the child is desperate for attention. In the child's mind, whatever the attention they received, they have unconsciously associated it with Love. And, it is this kind of attention that, unless healing occurs, the child will seek in adulthood.

The association with whatever the child experienced as Love, can lead a person to repeatedly choose the same kind of partner, hoping that the outcome would be different. Such a pattern has been called Repetition Compulsion, and sadly, it is experienced by many.

There is a part of our ego that lives in fantasy. This ego-fantasy wants to believe that, like in the story of Sleeping Beauty, our prince or princess will come, and with one kiss, will awaken us from our unconscious slumber, and we will live, regardless of our past experiences, in Love happily ever after together. Of course, this is just a fairytale.

The journey to find an Unconditional, Loving, Soul-Partnership relationship is profoundly rewarding, but it takes work, attention and a maturing of the ego. It doesn't happen all by itself. Because it lives so deep in our unconscious, freeing ourselves from Repetition Compulsion requires a lot of focused healing effort. And, for most of us, overcoming it without a trusted, capable guide is unlikely. But, to live in the fullness of a relationship, overcome it, we must.

What Is a Soul Partner?

A Soul Partner is, above all, a person who is ready, willing, able, and growing in the capacity to give and receive Unconditional, Universal Great-Love. A soul partner is developing self-awareness and responsiveness and is able to give and receive input. Unquestionably, both partners must have the inner strength and trust to be vulnerable, open and intimate. Both partners are learning how to go beyond judgment and take personal accountability for the experiences of their lives.

We consciously prepare for a Soul-Partnership. It is a choice that both partners make. It is not something that one person luckily finds, like a four-leaf clover. It also involves ongoing work that a couple does individually and together. It is something into which they grow.

I do not believe that we have only one perfect person who could be our Soul-Partner. There might be many people we meet along the way who could give and receive Unconditional Great-Love in a profoundly fulfilling manner. The Soul Partner's job is not to carry you off into the sunset of a perfect, frictionless relationship. The Soul-Partner's job is to be an Unconditionally Loving and dependable catalyst for your growth while tending to their own. And vice-versa.

Soul-Partnering is a blend of Unconditional Love and personal preference. While many couples might Love without judgment, Unconditional Love alone is not enough motivation to keep a relationship together. There has to be enough commonality to enrich the relationship. There also needs to be a mutuality of tastes and interests. And, for most couples, there has to be chemistry; sexual attraction for most couples is a fundamental element in keeping a relationship together and lively.

How Can We Prepare for Soul-Partnering?

Love yourself. It sounds easy enough, yet this can be quite a challenge for some, if not, most people. We have been socially conditioned to judge, criticize, and beat up on ourselves when we don't meet someone else's arbitrary standards. We may have come to believe that Love is conditional, and that we have to earn Love by behaving, excelling and performing.

How do we know if we do, or do not Love ourselves? We demonstrate Self-Love in how we react when we make a mistake, fail at something or hurt someone. If we can observe this behavior with compassion and as a learning opportunity, rather than beating ourselves up, then this is Self-Love.

Furthermore, every feeling, whether positive or negative, we have about someone else, reflects how we feel about some part of ourselves. Any block to Universal Great-Love stems from a restriction upon Self-Love.

First, if we can become aware of our feelings about others, we can use these observations to explore our limits to Self-Love. We can lovingly ask ourselves, *"If all of my feelings about others reflect some insecurity or limitation I have about myself, what can I learn from all my judgments?"*

Consider the uncomfortable feeling of jealousy. Perhaps jealousy connects you to a feeling of victimization, a sense that you have somehow been, or will be, cheated on or deceived. Jealousy could enflame a feeling of not being good enough for your partner, the fear that your partner secretly longs to be with someone thinner, more prosperous or more attractive.

Holding onto jealousy and victimization will eventually lead you to project it onto a partner. It will serve you, and a Soul-Partnership, to explore the perspective that every challenge and uncomfortable feeling we face is there to help us grow.

What about the feeling of blame? Blaming others usually grows out of our sense of insufficiency and lack of self-worth. We blame others when there is not enough room to face our blame when there is not enough self-esteem in ourselves.

When these feelings come up, look for the part of yourself that feels wounded and vulnerable. Usually, this is related to childhood experiences, and this inner child in you may want others to also feel wrong and bad.

In reality, these uncomfortable feelings and judgments are just memory-charged emotions that remain in your unconscious, begging for your Love.

When your hurt Inner Child and unconscious get the Love it needs, it heals more quickly and thoroughly. When you have healed, you end up feeling compassion for another rather than blame.

Can you imagine how this transformation would benefit a Soul-Partnership?

Withholds to Self-Love sometimes come from within us, and sometimes they are feelings taken unconsciously from our parents, grandparents, our ancestral lineage, social conditioning and religion. When this happens, it can be difficult to know what is ours and what is others.

It is challenging to clear out our own hurts, misperceptions and retained emotions. However, it is more effortless, and much quicker to release the carried emotions of others. Releasing them can sometimes be done in minutes.

If you are noticeably empathic, this is an ability you will want to learn sooner than later.

Quotes on Romance, Intimacy, and Love

"I'm not telling you it is going to be easy – I am telling you it is going to be worth it."

~Art Williams

"Romantic love is an illusion. Most of us discover the truth at the end of a love affair or else when the sweet emotions of love lead us into marriage and then turn down their flames."

~Thomas Moore

"There are no goodbyes for us. Wherever you are, you will always be in my heart."

~Mahatma Gandhi

"Finding intimacy begins with discovering ourselves, not with fixing or controlling ourselves or our partners. We have to be visible before we can be seen."

~Jett Psaris and Marlena S Lyons

"The beginning of Love is to let those we love be perfectly themselves, and not to twist them to fit our own image. Otherwise, we love only the reflection of ourselves we find in them."

~Thomas Merton

"Don't ever think I fell for you, or fell over you. I didn't fall in Love, I rose in it."

~Toni Morrison

"Nothing can come between us Cathy, not even you."

~Heathcliff

"Far too many people are looking for the right person, instead of trying to be the right person."

~Gloria Steinem

"There is a paradox at the heart of human unfolding: We can only love others to the degree that we are capable of loving ourselves. But, on the other hand, we are not born loving ourselves. We develop self-love by internalizing the love of all those who have loved us. As infants, we do not make our own food; neither do we make our own love."

~Dennis Rivers

"There is only one happiness in this life, to love and be loved."

~George Sand

"I'm selfish, impatient, and a little insecure. I make mistakes, I am out of control and at times hard to handle. But if you can't handle me at my worst, then you sure as hell don't deserve me at my best."

~Marilyn Monroe

"Since every adult has things to work on, refusal to work is the equivalent of reluctance to relate as an adult. And if a reasonable amount of work has been done and no change has resulted, the relationship is ready to be released so both parties can move on. Some relationships will never work, and when we waste our energy trying to rejuvenate them, we simply end up feeling depleted."

~David Richo

"Under cherry blossoms

Who is anymore

A stranger?"

~Kobayashi Issa

"Relationships blossom when you and I become an us."

~Rick Moss

4. Spiritual Growth

Relationships play a central part in Spiritual growth. Rarely does one's path lead away from society altogether. And even for the monk, nun, or recluse, there is often a Spiritual Guide or mentor.

Relationships reveal to us the nature of our unconscious. Because of the obscure nature of the unconscious, we often don't know what we are thinking or feeling at the unconscious level. Our interactions with people make our unconscious emotions and issues manifest, especially people we are close to or connected with through work or family.

People become screens upon which our unconscious projects our unhealed thoughts and emotions. These unhealed and hidden issues are barriers to our ability to Love and to react without judgment. Bringing consciousness to these unhealed and unconscious issues is of immense value to our Spiritual growth.

Spiritual growth almost always requires a teacher, master, Spiritual Director or guru. Guidance is required because almost all of the mind is unavailable to our conscious awareness. The teachers' job is to help us bring clarity and Light to our minds. Without this insight, we will most likely stay stuck in our patterns and limitations.

A fundamental approach to breaking free of patterns and limitations is the ability and willingness to surrender. The more attached we are to our thoughts, opinions, and desires, the more our ego is in charge. An enlightened teacher observes our attachments, and leads us in a way that liberates our consciousness from egoic control.

Often, such a teacher will ask their student to do things that make no sense to the student. One teacher is well known for asking students to dig a swimming pool. Upon completion, he asked them to fill it and dig it somewhere else. Another master instructed students to address, stamp, and mail invitations to an event that was already over.

Relationship With the Divine

We can't see God or the "Ground of Being" with our human eyes. But, we can see the manifestation of the Divine in everything that we do see. As our Spiritual awareness grows, we enter into a relationship with the Divine by honoring and loving all of creation.

Maharishi Mahesh Yogi once said, "God comes to shake the hand of the man [person] who appreciates His creation." In our Love and appreciation, our relationship with the Divine becomes fuller and more interactive. Love opens the door to God.

In the maturity of our relationship with the Divine, we experience the Divine in everyone and everything.

Quotes About Spiritual Growth

"A soul mates purpose is to shake you up, tear apart your ego a little bit, show you your obstacles and addictions, break your heart open so new light can get in, to make you so desperate and out of control that you have to transform your life, then introduce you to your spiritual master…"

~Elizabeth Gilbert

"Trying to eliminate worldly temptations only makes our spiritual growth more limited."

~Toba Beta

"What lies behind us and what lies before us are small matters compared to what lies within us."

~Ralph Waldo Emerson

"The development of self then leads to a more fundamental level, the discovery of true self. This is the discovery that the positive qualities of character that spiritual life works so hard to cultivate are already present as our true nature."

~Jack Kornfield

"Practice kindness and harmlessness as if it were the greatest form of bliss and it will be."

~Tibetan Buddhist saying

"But if you accept that the relationship is here to make you conscious instead of happy, then the relationship will offer you salvation, and you will be aligning yourself with the higher consciousness that wants to be born into this world."

~Eckhart Tolle

"You can either be a host to God or a hostage to your ego. It's your call."

~Wayne Dyer

"God came to my house and asked for charity, And I fell on my knees and cried, "Beloved, what may I give?" "Just love, He said. "Just love."

~Rumi *(Translated by Daniel Ladinsky)*

An Integration

Let's state this poetically: "Walk with me, my Soul. Please help me to understand the value and purpose of relationships." And the Soul says, "Relationships are what makes us human. No one comes into this world but through a mother. Everyone will value themselves initially by how much this mother loves them. And then, they must come to Love themselves regardless of their experiences".

"In a perfect world, your father and mother's role would be to Love you with respect for your individuality. In the perfection of this world, your parents' role is to deliver to you the behavior that will activate your healing plan for this lifetime.

Neglectful, abusive, judgmental, critical, unpleasant though they may have been, they are exactly what and who you needed to experience in order to grow. It is through this plan you can learn to Love yourself exactly as you are." "Until a Soul comes to Love itself, It will not fully allow itself to Love or be Loved by another. Until the door has been opened by Self-Love, all relationships are limited and of a healing nature."

"Once there is enough Self-Love, then all relationships become avenues through which Love streams into the Soul. Once there is Self-Love, God's Love streams into the Soul from every person we meet. When Self-Love is full, everyone is experienced as Divine, and everyone is immersed in an ocean of Love." "This is the blessing that relationships offer."

In Essence

Everything in creation is in a relationship with everything else.

Distance is not a factor.

Everything is a manifestation of the One.

The more we grow and evolve, the less we judge, and the more we Love.

All of life, being part of the One, comes to us through relationships to help us discover who we really are. And through relationships, we have the Divine opportunity to realize who everyone and everything is as well.

Chapter 11

HEALING

Body, Mind and Soul

The separation between body and mind, although assumed by many, is in reality, superficial. It would be more beneficial to consider it the body/mind. This chapter will embrace a more holistic perspective and treat the body/mind and Soul as interrelated.

The body is the mind made manifest and writ large. The feedback loop between the body and mind is so integrated and complex, that this interpenetration is almost impossible to ignore. For healing to be profound, this body/mind integration needs to be respected.

To isolate the body as the source of disease and ignore the mind overlooks what the root of the word "healing" connotes: to make whole. It will be rewarding to examine how our minds can create sickness and isolation, or support health and Wholeness.

In honoring our integrated Wholeness, we access our potential and broaden the scope of our ability to heal; and the Soul cannot be left out of this Wholeness.

Many believe that the Soul is an individualized creation of God created to support our growth and ultimate enlightenment. In my practice, I have seen that there are diseases that spring from unhealed aspects of the Soul. These Soul-based distortions find expression in the body/mind and must be addressed and healed at the Soul level. And, healing doesn't stop at the level of the Soul.

Spirit is the part of the Self that transcends individuality. Spirit expresses the Divine, God, if you will. Spirit is the Source of all that is Good in our lives. Just as it is limited to envisioning the body as separate from the mind, it is short-sighted to conceive of humans without our Source and Spirit's role in our healing and wellbeing.

In this chapter, we will explore the body/mind, Soul and Spirit as they relate to healing. We'll examine what healing is and the possibility that we might unconsciously be resisting the healing we seek.

Body/Mind

The body and mind indeed appear to be two individual aspects of ourselves. Many Doctors and other care-providing professionals still treat them as distinct, and do not consider the interrelatedness when providing care to one or the other.

There is, however, a vast body of evidence to support interacting not just with the body, or solely with the mind, but with the body/mind. The study of stress is a perfect example of body/mind interconnection.

Stress

Stress is a body/mind issue. It is an accepted fact that stress is a factor in most physical dysfunction. Many estimate that it is a major factor in

95% of diseases. A key aspect of stress is mental. How the mind perceives an event is central to how the body will react to it. Over 20 years of research has demonstrated that physical health improves when stress is reduced through meditation and other modalities.

When stressed due to a physical or emotional challenge, our body releases adrenaline and cortisol. These hormones help us to meet challenging or dangerous situations. But, stress can continue after the seeming threat is gone, and the body can continue to release these hormones. This continued stress response results in a weakened immune system, reduced healing rate and digestive problems. (Source: Florida Medical Clinic – "What is the Mind-Body Connection")

Pain

The intimate connection between mind and body is also apparent in how physical issues like pain or disability affect our mental state. Physical pain often leads to mental conditions like depression, loss of enthusiasm and even suicide. However, when emotional states receive appropriate attention, physical pain is often significantly reduced.

Negative and Positive Thinking

Negative thinking is another widely-recognized source of health problems. Assuming a negative outcome, self-judgment, or lack of forgiveness are just a few of the mental/emotional patterns that negatively, and profoundly impact our health, causing depression, weakening our immunity and contributing to addictions. On the other hand, positive thinking increases a sense of wellbeing, and offers other physiological benefits, including cardiovascular health (Source: thehealthplace.com).

Positive thinking generates brain chemistry that can lower blood pressure, reduce the risk of heart disease, strengthen the immune system, reduce insomnia and back pain and change your thinking about the future. (Source: Michigan Medicine, UofMhealth.org).

Emotions Are Stored in the Body

Profound and damaging emotional experiences are stored throughout the body/mind, and until they are released and healed, they affect our mental, emotional and physical welfare. Many writers and researchers call the body the home of the subconscious. Candace Pert has written extensively about how emotions are triggered at the level of the cells. The brain sends out chemical messages that, when received at the cell's specific receptor sites, stimulate our emotions.

To summarize, the body and mind are interrelated. If there is disease or dysfunction, there is always a mental or emotional component that needs attention. On the other hand, to maximize our health, we can use positive thinking, visualization, and prayer to support our physical wellbeing.

There is a wonderful story in the Washington Post from October 21, 1986, written by Don Colburn that illustrates the powerful influence of positive thinking and feeling about an experience by Norman Cousins. Cousins recovered from Degenerative Collagen Illness - a severe, life-threatening disease of the connective tissue.

While in the hospital healing from this disease, he discovered that laughter can help to heal. Cousins discovered that 10 minutes of deep, belly laughter resulted in hours of pain-free sleep.

He wrote about his path to recovery through laughter in the highly successful book titled *"Anatomy of an Illness"*. He went on to join the faculty of the University of California at Los Angeles School of Medicine, researching and teaching about the biochemistry of emotions.

Quotes About Body/Mind

"Western medicine still makes serious distinctions between mental, emotional and physical roots of illnesses despite the amassing of research that finds that mind and body are so interwoven that such distinctions are not only artificial, they're unscientific."

~Herbert Benson, MD

"Every problem is primarily mental..."

~Ernest Holmes

"...The body developed out of us, not we from it."

~Mewlana Jalaluddin Rumi

"Learn to read symptoms not only as problems to be overcome but as messages to be heeded."

~Gabor Maté

"Where the mind goes, the body will follow."

~Arnold Schwarzenegger

"The body is the outermost layer of the mind."

~David Mitchell

"It is the mind itself which builds the body."

~Joseph Pilates

"There is no illness of the body except for the mind."

~Socrates

"Before you heal the body you must first heal the mind."

~Aristotle

"Your body is your subconscious mind and you can't heal it by talk alone."

~Candace Pert

What Is Healing?

Healing goes beyond the elimination of a symptom. Symptom elimination could be called curing. An example of this would be, the taking of pain medicine to make a headache go away.

Healing is more than addressing a physical problem solely at the physical level. Profound healing must also address the relevant mental and emotional issues that contribute to the problem that has manifested through the body.

For example, a client of mine had severe digestive issues. Medical treatment alone wasn't producing results. Digestion was improved when he addressed his childhood fears. Yet, sometimes, medical and psychological treatment must turn to a higher source beyond the mind.

When the world-famous psychiatrist, Carl Jung, faced an alcoholic patient he could not help, he sent this patient home to have a spiritual experience. Jung saw that spiritual "medicine" was the only available course of healing for the addiction. And, it worked wonders; not only for the patient, but this spiritual experience became the catalyst for the creation of Alcoholics Anonymous.

In the thirty years of my practice, I have never worked with a physical issue that did not have mental and emotional elements. In many cases, with the healing of the mental and emotional issues, the physical symptoms disappeared. And, the quest for healing doesn't stop at the level of Body/Mind.

It is not unusual for physical or emotional challenges to spring from unresolved issues at the Soul level. Dramatic changes can occur very quickly when we have healed past life issues held at the Soul level. In order to be complete, Healing needs to bring Body, Mind and Soul into harmony and union. Union requires the help and blessings of Spirit, which is Wholeness in and of itself.

Quotes About What Is Healing and Why Illness Can Serve Us

"But healing and curing are inherently different. Curing means "eliminating all evidence of disease," while healing means "becoming whole.""

~Lissa Rankin, M.D.

"Healing will always stand aside when it would be seen as a threat."

~A Course in Miracles

To understand this idea, imagine that the only time a child felt kindness and attention was when they were sick. This person may consciously or unconsciously conclude that they have to be sick to feel loved and cared for. Getting well then could be seen as a threat, not a promise. Another person could hold the unconscious thought that they have to carry their parent's disease, and if they got better, their parents would get sick and maybe die. Healing, in these cases, will need to include psychological and emotional attention as well as a new understanding.

"All healing is essentially the release from fear."

~A Course in Miracles

"Healing is the effect of minds that join, as sickness comes from minds that separate."

~A Course in Miracles

"Healing: to touch or to enter with mercy and awareness those areas of ourselves from which we have withdrawn in anger or judgment."

~Stephen Levine

"The body is a self-healing organism, so it's really about clearing things out of the way so the body can heal itself."

~Barbara Brennan

"The wound is the place where the Light enters you."

~Rumi

"The depth of the wound has a relationship to the height or expansiveness of the gift."

~Jeffrey Van Dyk

"It has been said, 'time heals all wounds.' I do not agree. The wounds remain. In time, the mind, protecting its sanity, covers them with scar tissue and the pain lessened. But it is never gone."

~Rose Fitzgerald Kennedy

"Wounds do not need to be gone to serve us. They can motivate us to seek solace and peace in what is unchanging, in what is always Whole."

~Rick Moss

"Nothing ever goes away until it has taught us what we need to know."

~Pema Chödrön

"Our wounds are often the openings into the best and most beautiful part of us."

~David Richo

"We are healed of a suffering only by experiencing it to the full."

~Marcel Proust

"You cannot free yourself from what you can't see. What you are conditioned to push away and not look at is reflected back to you in what is called "the outside environment."

~Devaji

"By far the strongest poison to the human spirit is the inability to forgive oneself or another person. Forgiveness is no longer an option but a necessity for healing."

~Caroline Myss

"There can be no healing without Teaching…"

Dr. D.D. Palmer

"Healing is an inside job."

~Dr. B.J. Palmer

"The body is the most visible form of the unconscious."

~Carl Jung

Quotes About How We Say 'No" to Healing

"Almost every major illness that people acquire has been linked to chronic stress."

~Dr. Bruce Lipton

"The more you repeat a particular neural pathway, the more it becomes fixed…nerves cells that fire together wire together…"

~Dr. Candace Pert

"It's as if the king sent you into a far and distant land with one specific task to accomplish. You can accomplish a hundred other things but if you fail to accomplish the one thing for which you have been sent, it will be as if you have done nothing."

~Rumi

Rumi believes that everyone has a guiding purpose to their lives, also called dharma. If we are not discovering this purpose, the disease could be a way of getting our attention.

"Remember, you have been criticizing yourself for years and it hasn't worked. Try approving of yourself and see what happens."

~Louise Hay

Quotes About How We Can Say "Yes" to Healing

Healing is, in effect, "a treatment for incorrect thinking."

~Ernest Holmes

"The first step in healing or recovery must involve awareness of where your past and injuries are stored, and then making an attempt to unravel them."

~Dr. Candace Pert

"Your number one indicator for how healthy you'll be and how long you'll live is your level of self-esteem and self-worth."

~Dr. Candace Pert

"…there isn't any absolute or external reality! What you experience as reality is your story of what happened."

~Dr. Candace Pert

"Positive thoughts have a profound effect on behavior and genes but *only* when they are in harmony with subconscious programming."

~Dr. Bruce Lipton

"We lose the present moment and condemn ourselves to living in the past when we rush. The Goodness, Power and Light of the present moment is the very basis of healing."

~Rick Moss

Healing the Soul

Our Soul is our God-created vehicle that maintains our uniqueness from lifetime to lifetime. It contains both the unlearned lessons from the past and unresolved karma from past actions. The Soul also is the home of our Divine qualities like Compassion, Kindness, and Love that come abundantly from God, our Creator.

Spiritual Master Paramahamsa Vishwananda expresses it beautifully when he describes the Soul as bound by karma, and covered by layers of shadow and shade, which, when removed, reveals Spirit – the Spirit of God. He states that "Spirit is the indweller of the Soul".

How are these shadows and shades removed? We return to heal and transform karma. We do this through meditation, purification, learning, inner work, devotional activity, and actions that spring from Love and conscious awareness. This evolution is the whole curriculum of classroom earth.

When the Soul is overburdened, dark, and avoiding its pain with addictions, healing must reach the Soul before we can heal the Body/Mind. Issues of guilt, shame, blame, and judgment need to be addressed. Self-Love will be required. Self-realization, and the healing of the Soul will be impossible without Unconditional Love.

In 30 years of practice, I have seen the remains of past life experiences and traumas held in the Soul, just waiting for the opportunity to be healed. These past life wounds are what we could call diseases of the Soul. The wounds are the result of past life traumatic and abusive experiences.

In order to heal, the Soul needs to realize and experience why these lifetimes occurred, and how they are a part of our healing and growth. Past Lifetime experiences are always pointing us in the direction of forgiveness, learning and Love.

In my practice, I have witnessed clients with multiple lifetimes dealing with the same issue. This issue might be powerlessness, or, may have power over others. Or, it might be an inability to control their desires. Such issues that have occurred over lifetimes can often be positively influenced by treating them in their entirety rather than by approaching each life individually.

This multi-lifetime approach might parallel the Sanskrit term of a vāsanā. A vāsanā is an impression held in the unconscious that influences future behavior. I believe a vāsanā can exist at the soul level.

The Soul's reaction to the early moments of its creation is another disease of the Soul. When the Soul first experiences itself as separate from its Creator, it may interpret its separative experience as something it did wrong. When this happens, there is a multi-lifetime pattern of "I've done something wrong" or "I'm bad."

A second distortion producing a response to separation is "You have done this to me. I'm a victim". The Soul blames God and everyone else for victimizing it.

These two primary misperceptions that linger at the Soul level require support and healing when the Soul is incarnated and on the earth. It is profoundly helpful when a loving, knowledge guide can help the Soul release these traumatic misperceptions of its first moments.

Quotes About Healing the Soul

"There may come a time when the burden that the body is carrying for the heart and spirit is too burdensome; when the sorrow, resentment, judgment and grief floods and overwhelms the body's ability to heal itself. It is then that the wise doctor points his or her patient in a different direction. Carl Jung offered us a perfect demonstration of this when he told his alcoholic patient he had to leave and return to the United States and have a spiritual experience. His patient did this and it worked and his experience became central to the work and success of Alcoholics Anonymous."

~Ernest Kurtz and Katherine Ketcham

"When a man attains full control of his mind, his bodily cells and parts may be replaced or changed as often as desired, and at will."

~Paramahansa Yogananda

"There is no way out, there is still always a way through. So don't turn away from the pain. Face it. Feel it fully…Stay alert, stay present – present with your whole Being, with every cell of your body. As you do, you are bringing a light into the darkness. This is the flame of your consciousness."

~Eckhart Tolle

"Healing begins with the repair of emotional injuries…Healing is an active and internal process that includes investigating one's attitudes, memories, and beliefs with the desire to release all negative patterns that prevent one's full emotional and spiritual recovery."

~Caroline Myss, Ph.D.

"Healing does not mean going back to the way things were before, but rather allowing what is now to move us closer to God."

~Ram Dass

Spirit or God As the Source of Healing

All healing has its source in God or Spirit. God is the source of all that is Good. The Love that God is, heals. The Presence that God is, heals.

Where there is a perception of alienation from God or Spirit, the result will be mental, emotional or physical disease. All issues that our egos hold against God are projections of our own, what I call "unhealedness". When we address these judgments, resentments, and misunderstandings, healing occurs.

Quotes About Spirit or God As the Source of Healing

"Your mind can be possessed by illusions, but spirit is eternally free."

~A Course in Miracles

"Any illness is a direct message to you that tells you how you have not been loving who you are, cherishing yourself in order to be who you are. This is the basis of all healing."

~Barbara Brennan

"…More needs she the divine than the physician."

Shakespeare

"When you discover the innate innocence in you, you discover the innate innocence in everything."

~Devaji

"As you become more aware of what gets you to God and what doesn't, you will naturally let go of what doesn't."

~Ram Dass

"All conditions can be treated by spiritual healing – but not all people. Some people are more receptive than others to this treatment, due to a number of factors such as karma and mental outlook."

~The Aetherius Society

"If spiritual healing does not appear to be working, it will be valuable to explore our egoic resistance."

~Rick Moss

If we believe as I do, that all Love comes from God, Love, then, is spiritual healing.

~Rick Moss

"Calmness of mind is one of the beautiful jewels of wisdom. When you are calm, having learned how to govern your own emotions, how to govern your own mind, you know how to access the gifts of the universe."

~James Allen

An Integration

In our Wholeness, we experience that we are not a body; we are not our egoic mind; we are not even the Soul.

In our Wholeness, we transcend all parts, all fixities, all limitations.

In our Wholeness, we realize that we are Spirit and that everything we experience is Spirit as well. From Wholeness comes health.

In Essence

Eckhart Tolle writes, "Focus your attention on the Now and tell me what problem you have at this moment."

We can step out of the past when we step out of our thinking mind, and enter the present moment through our bodies. When we are focused and present, our Body/Mind and Soul are connected. The body thrives in the present moment. And it is there that we need to meet it.

We can give our body attention if it is in pain or in need. We listen to it rather than trying to put it out of our awareness.

If we listen to our body, it will talk to us. It may tell us how ignored it feels, how unimportant. Perhaps it will reveal how judged it feels. Our Body/Mind and Soul is asking for Love and attention, for acceptance and respect. Perhaps it is asking for a specific healing modality.

And, if we keep listening, keep holding Loving awareness, the body may give up many hurts and traumas that it has held; because, up till now, it may well have believed that we didn't care.

Loving our Body/Mind, exactly as it is in this present moment, is a form of transformational healing, and it leads us to Wholeness, and the realization of Spirit as our Divine nature.

Chapter 12

GRATITUDE

Opening the Heart,
Enriching Your Life, Freeing Your Soul

G ratitude is one thing we can learn to do right now that has profound emotional, physical, interpersonal, and spiritual benefits. Gratitude enhances physical and emotional health. Sleep and self-esteem improves in gratitude. We feel happy when we are grateful.

Those in the state of Gratitude-for-Everything live in harmony and acceptance of all that happens in their lives. They live in peace. There are so many rewards; yet, gratitude can also be extremely challenging to the ego regardless of the benefits.

To the ego, gratitude is an insult to unaddressed painful emotions from the past.

Self-Inquiry Questions

- How might experiencing gratitude make you feel vulnerable?

- Could you imagine an experience of freedom that Gratitude-for-Everything might give you?

- How might feeling gratitude change your relationship with others?

- In what way is gratitude a prayer?

The Ego Is Inherently Ungrateful

In the quintessential American success story, someone given nothing pulls themselves up by their bootstraps and makes something of themselves. It is an achievement that fosters pride. The famous Horatio Alger "rags to riches" story is a prime example.

In contrast, a person to whom a wealthy parent or grandparent gives everything is looked down upon, even despised.

In one study, over one-third of American men reported a preference for concealing feelings of gratitude. The comic character of Bart Simpson personifies a negative attitude toward gratitude. When asked to say grace in one episode, he says, "Dear God, we paid for all of this stuff ourselves, so thanks for nothing."

To the ego, gratitude brings up indebtedness, dependency, resentment, vulnerability and humility.

Cultural Superstitions

Superstitions can run deep in our unconscious and the collective unconscious. They can have profound influences of which we may be completely unaware, making a choice to be grateful even more difficult. Here are a few examples:

Chinese peasant farmers have been known to go out to the rice patties; and even if the rice is good, they would say, "Bad rice, bad rice," to trick the gods into not destroying their bountiful harvest.

"Knock on wood" derives from a pagan belief that malevolent spirits inhabited wood, and if you expressed a hope for the future, you should touch or knock on wood to prevent the spirits from hearing and preventing your wishes from coming true.

As a result of centuries of persecution, some Jews may avoid showing off things considered to be too good, or acknowledge good things for fear that jealous people would give them the evil eye (kinahora), and somebody might harm them. In the past, parents would talk about their children as ugly so that the gods wouldn't be jealous.

Gratitude as a Choice

Most of us experience flashes of gratitude. Perhaps we receive an unexpected gift, expressions of affection, or an advancement in our career. But, like the pleasant new car smell, it evaporates rather quickly.

Our brains give negative feelings far greater attention than positive ones. This well-documented fact is called the negative bias of the brain. Negative feelings like fear, anger and grievances are more directly related to survival than joy and happiness. Our brain's primary job is to keep us alive.

We are not victims of the tendencies of our brains. We have the innate ability to make a positive choice that overrides negative thinking. We do not have to choose Gratitude just once. It is a decisive and focused decision that we must repeatedly make if we are to reap its rewards. Our brains support us when we choose gratitude.

Neuro-Science

Gratitude profoundly lights up the brain. Our brains light up just by searching for something to be grateful for. The antidepressant Wellbutrin, boosts the neurotransmitter and pleasure enhancer dopamine – so does gratitude. Prozac boosts the neurotransmitter and happiness enhancer serotonin. So does gratitude.

Trying to think of things that inspire gratitude forces you to focus on positive things in your life. This simple act increases serotonin in the anterior cingulate cortex.

Study after study has shown a profound association with higher levels of gratitude and wellbeing with more fulfilling relationships, better sleep, greater resilience, and protection from stress and depression.

Experiential Opportunity: Exploring Your Resistance to Gratitude

A fearful, insecure ego resists gratitude. The ego feels a sense of control and power when it is rewarded for something it feels it has accomplished. To receive without earning can bring up feelings of shame and is a humbling experience to the ego.

You can use the following exercise to explore your egoic resistance to gratitude. Please remember that you are not your ego. You are the unchanging, expanded Wholeness that is the Self.

Scenario 1: Your least favorite parent gives you a significant gift. Write down as many responses from your ego as you can. (For example, it makes me feel like a child. Or, this won't make up for the past.)

Scenario 2: Two people you know in the company you work for are given advancement and raises. You have not. Write down the feelings that come up. (For example, it's not fair. I feel so jealous! What's wrong with me?)

Scenario 3: It's Thanksgiving. You are at the home of your spouse's family, which you don't particularly like. Or, you are alone for Thanksgiving. Feel the emotions that fill you. (For example, Do you have any room in the above scenarios for gratitude? Or, do you feel dominated by other emotions? What are they?)

Could you pay attention to those feelings, allow them to be felt, and then acknowledge: this is how a part of me feels?

Is there another part of me with which I can access feelings of gratitude regardless of the circumstances? This is not pretending; it is refocusing.

A Process: Making More Room for Gratitude

We may obscure, repress and consider feelings of gratitude unjustified if we have known neglect, abuse, or felt unloved as a child.

In the event that we were not loved and didn't feel taken care of as children, it may be difficult to feel gratitude until the work is done to heal the past and experience our childhood from a growth and development perspective.

See chapter 3, "Healing the Wounded Child Within" for more detail on the Inner Child Process.

1. Imagine an inner child at a time in their home where they didn't feel safe or loved. Find a kind and caring part of yourself to extend to this child. If you're having trouble, perhaps think of a sleeping child or a pet or a person for which you deeply care.

2. Can this kind, caring part of you imagine harming while at the same time feeling this care and love? If not, then direct this care and love to the child in the room.

3. As the loving part (we'll call this your Best-Self), go to the room where the child sits alone, and ask if you can sit with them.

4. Tell the child that you have come to love and protect them. Imagine spending time giving positive attention, kindness, and care.

5. Tell the child Love has sent you to be their Loving Adult and that you are not going to go away – ever (If the word "ever" scares you, know that the adult is talking about this moment as infinite. But the child needs to think of it as an expression of "always"). Everyone is meant to have one person to love and protect them, 24/7; and I am that person for you.

6. Imagine days, weeks, months and years passing with you there being consistently loving and protective. Can you get a sense that this growing child would be more and more open to gratitude, while before, they were closed to gratitude?

Quotes About the Power of Gratitude.

"No amount of regret can change the past. No amount of anxiety can change the future. Any amount of gratitude can change the present."

~Author unknown

"If the only prayer you said was thank you, that would be enough."

~Meister Eckhart

"We can only be said to be alive in those moments when our hearts are conscious of our treasures."

~Thornton Wilder

"Gratitude opens the door to the power, the wisdom, the creativity of the Universe. You open the door through gratitude."

~Deepak Chopra

"When you are grateful – when you can see what you have – you unlock blessings to flow in your life."

~Suze Orman

"Gratitude is not only the greatest of virtues but the parent of all the others."

~Cicero

"What separates privilege from entitlement is gratitude."

Brené Brown

"Wear gratitude like a cloak and it will feed every corner of your life."

~Rumi

"Gratitude is the sweetest thing in a seeker's life – in all human life. If there is gratitude in your heart, there will be tremendous sweetness in your eyes."

~Sri Chinmoy

"The essence of all beautiful art, all great art, is gratitude."

~Friedrich Nietzsche

"The roots of all goodness lie in the soil of appreciation for goodness."

~H.H Dalai Lama

"When it comes to life, the critical thing is whether you take things for granted or take them with gratitude."

~G. K. Chesterton

"Giving thanks has a way of magically reducing the charge we hold around things and people."

~Stephanie Bennett Vogt

"When you appreciate the good, the good appreciates."

~Dr. Tal Ben Shahar

"We can complain because rose bushes have thorns or rejoice that thorn bushes have roses"

~ Abraham Lincoln

"Piglet noticed that even though he had a Very Small Heart, it could hold a rather large amount of Gratitude."

~A.A. Milne

The Experience of Pure Gratitude: For All Things

Can you find within yourself the feeling of being grateful for something or someone? Now, can you let go of the object of your gratitude, and just be aware of gratitude itself?

Perhaps a good word for this experience might be unconditional or transcendent gratitude, or gratitude for no reason.

You might feel an openness or expansion. You might experience a kind of vibratory hum.

However, you might feel that the word devotion does not quite fit when applied to meaningful feelings or kindness; perhaps gratitude does.

A Gratitude-For-All-Things Exercise

1. Close your eyes.
2. Take five slow, peaceful, relaxing breaths.
3. Let tension drain out your feet into the earth.
4. Envision it transmuted to life-force.
5. Imagine being held in an embrace of kindness, compassion, and Love.
6. Receive these words from a non-judgmental Loving Source: "Nothing you have ever done and nothing you could ever do will reduce the Love I feel for you by even one drop. Everything you have experienced is bringing you closer to Me."
7. Just smile at that part of your ego-mind that wants to dispute that gift of Love for a few moments.

8. How grateful do you feel that you are Loved?

Quotes About Gratitude-For-All-Things

"Cultivate the habit of being grateful for every good thing that comes to you, and give thanks continuously. And because all things have contributed to your advancement, you should include all things in your gratitude."

~Ralph Waldo Emerson

"True forgiveness is when you can say, 'Thank you for that experience.'"

~Oprah Winfrey

"The feeling of rightness is inherent in the Self and independent of anything that appears to change."

~Devaji

"Give thanks in all circumstances; for this is God's will for you…"

1 Thessalonians 5:18 *(New International Version of the Bible)*

"Don't pray when it rains if you don't pray when the sun shines."

~Leroy "Satchel" Paige

"One joyfully realizes that Brahmin - the inconceivable, indescribable Reality - manifests as every step or level of experience, from the first to last."

~Ramakrishna

"If God said, 'Rumi, pay homage to everything that has helped you enter my arms,' there would not be one experience of my life, not one thought, not one feeling, not any act, I would not bow to."

~Rumi

An Integration

Thank you! Magic happens when we put gratitude into words and are nourished by our hearts. Our brain function changes, our heart opens and Love flows. Perhaps it is a mystical incantation.

This much we know: there is a world, perhaps a universe of rewards when we can bypass our ego's resistance to feeling grateful. We are encouraged to move in the direction of gratitude for everything in order to be open to this reward.

This, of course, requires that we trust that God, Spirit, or Life is presenting everything we experience as a gift for us and our growth.

What if we chose to embrace that idea, even for a moment? How beautifully we seem to move together! I ask myself, can I now dance with gratitude?

In Essence

In Gratitude we can find peace, happiness, wellbeing and greater health.

In blame, we find resentment and grievance, depression, alienation and sickness.

We can choose which path attracts us more.

If we choose gratitude, this is a choice we will need to make again and again.

Choosing gratitude, like all spiritual practice, requires dedication.

There are no limits to Love and Consciousness if we choose gratitude-for-all-things.

Chapter 13

GENUINE HAPPINESS

The Experience of Our Essential Nature

I t is our essential nature to seek ultimate and lasting happiness. Being aware of our core Self and our essence allows us to know who we really are. Vedic philosophy refers to this essential nature as Satcitananda – Being, Consciousness, Bliss. To experience this supreme happiness is to know that nothing compares to it. The True Self exists only in our experience, not in the world the ego knows.

Most people associate happiness with pleasure, derived from accomplishments, achievement, admiration, and other pleasant external life experiences.

The body is also a prime source of egoic or temporary happiness. Bodily pleasure can make us feel happy but is short-lived. The body becomes unresponsive when it is repeatedly exposed to the same stimulus.

We can also experience genuine happiness in our daily lives. We find inner-based happiness when we are in connection with something greater than ourselves. Perhaps it is a cause. Perhaps it is service. For many, it is a connection to the spiritual realm. Without fail, we experience giving and receiving Unconditional-Love as an unfailing path to happiness.

Self-Inquiry Questions

- What gives you the most lasting happiness?
- Do you often choose being right over being happy?
- Can you experience a connection between acceptance of whatever is and being happy?
- Do you know someone who is happy? What is the source of their happiness?

Quotes About the Nature of Happiness

"Happiness never decreases by being shared."

~Buddha

"If you want happiness for an hour, take a nap.

If you want happiness for a day, go fishing.

If you want happiness for a year, inherit a fortune.

If you want happiness for a lifetime, help somebody else."

~Chinese Proverb

"Others may know pleasure, but pleasure is not happiness. It has no more importance than a shadow following a man."

~Muhammad Ali

"Sometimes your joy is the source of your smile, but sometimes your smile is the source of your joy."

~Thich Nhat Hanh

"Happiness is when what you think, what you say, and what you do are in harmony."

~Mahatma Gandhi

"There is only one cause of unhappiness: the false beliefs you have in your head, beliefs so widespread, so commonly held, that it never occurs to you to question them."

~Anthony de Mello

"Happiness is having a large, loving, caring, close-knit family in another city."

~George Burns

"Happiness, not in another place, but this place, not for another hour, but this hour."

~Walt Whitman

"I am very happy because I have conquered myself and not the world. I am very happy because I have loved the world and not myself."

~Sri Chinmoy

"Success is getting what you want. Happiness is wanting what you get."

~Dale Carnegie

"Most folks are usually about as happy as they make up their minds to be."

~Abraham Lincoln

"You cannot protect yourself from sadness without protecting yourself from happiness."

~Jonathan Safran Foer

Our Unconscious Resistance to Happiness

Our unconscious is extremely powerful. Most people consciously believe that they want to be happy. But, if we are not truly happy, we will be greatly rewarded by examining our limiting beliefs and retained emotions. These stand like great boulders on the path to happiness.

Based on my experiences working with clients over several decades, I have provided a partial list of the unconscious (and sometimes conscious) reasons for resisting or rejecting happiness:

- ❖ I have to mirror my parents' emotional states (sadness, depression, grief, etc.) to feel a closer bond and be loved.

- ❖ I can't allow myself to surpass my parent(s). It would humiliate them.

- ❖ The world appears so unhappy, I wouldn't fit in if I were happy.

- ❖ The world will expect more of me if I am happy.

- ❖ When I'm unhappy, I feel more in control. Happiness is a vulnerability.

- ❖ I can punish my parents for how they treated me by being unhappy. It's a way of saying, "See what you did to me."

- ❖ I can punish others by being unhappy.

- ❖ I am unworthy of being happy.

- ❖ I can punish myself by being unhappy.

- ❖ If I'm too happy, I will be shattered, and something terrible will happen.

Making these beliefs as conscious as possible is one way to deal with them. When you are aware of the belief, think to yourself, "There I go again thinking that old thought." Then ask yourself, "Is this really true for me now?" "Do I need to keep trying to protect myself in this way?"

Inner child work can also be used to release limiting beliefs like these. This can be found in Chapter Three.

Increasing Our Capacity for Happiness

Happiness is an aspect of our essential nature; but, as we know, happiness is not our experience every moment.

There are three fundamental approaches to increasing our awareness and experience of happiness: Meditation, Mindset, and Love/Service/Gratitude.

Meditation

There are predominantly five well-known forms of Meditation: Transcendence-oriented Meditation (Transcendental Meditation™ (TM) and Sahaj Samadhi® are two of the most widely known forms), Mindfulness Meditation, Guided-Meditation, Meditative Contemplation, and Movement Meditation.

Transcendence-oriented Meditation is a technique that leads to the transcendence of personal awareness and an immersion in the field of Pure Consciousness. The meditator uses a mantra. The ultimate purpose of the mantra is to lose awareness of the mantra as it grows more subtle, and ultimately the mantra is lost in deeper awareness.

Scientific research on TM has repeatedly demonstrated that long-term meditators need much less-stimulus to experience authentic happiness. Additionally, long-term meditators feel a quantifiable reduction of anxiety and stress, and an increase in measures of wellbeing.

MindfulnessMeditation is a practice that helps a person stay present with what is. Buddhist master-teacher Thich Nhat Hanh writes, "The essence of our practice can be described as transforming suffering into happiness." Mindfulness Meditation, with full attention to what is, transforms suffering.

Mindfulness Meditation practice offers an expanded capacity to be aware of the present moment. Awareness of the in-and-out breath is central to the approach of Mindfulness.

There is a teaching story about a person who is sitting by a river. Their mind is filled with worry and concern. They cannot be present with the river because their mind imprisons them. The person is living in the past. Suddenly, a bird disturbs their thinking, and they watch the bird glide downstream, collecting a fish and taking flight.

We are not rewarded when we live in the past. Becoming present opens us up to possibilities we never saw before. The story concludes with a moral: We cannot catch real fish in the river of the mind, only when we are present to the Now moment.

Guided Meditation is a process in which one is led to having a particular experience. The recipient is guided to a quieter and more focused state of mind through voice, visualization, music, written word and insight. In this more open and receptive state, healing, understanding, release of old patterns, and transformation can occur.

Meditative Contemplation is a spiritually-focused exploration of an idea, question, or a specific situation. One uses thought to open the mind to deeper levels of thinking, feeling and insight. At the deeper levels of mind, there is greater peace, revelation and an expanded sense of connection.

Movement Meditation involves the intentional and conscious use of movement to center the practitioner within themselves and in peace. Actions might include yoga, walking slowly with full consciousness, qigong, tai chi, or immersion in nature.

Mindset is how we think about what we experience and how we think about the world around us. Both are central to our happiness; because, through thinking, we give meaning to our experiences. And through meaning, we generate our emotions. Happiness will not be possible if we believe that this world is a horrible place where 'terrible' things can happen at any moment.

On the other hand, fear and judgment are reduced if we believe that the world is our classroom, and we mature due to all of our experiences, including what we perceive as good and bad. In this state, it is much easier to find our way to happiness.

Love and Gratitude are two of the most powerful paths to happiness. When you combine the two, happiness cannot be resisted. When our hearts are open, the outflow of Love is so enlivening that everything is a source of happiness. When the addition of Gratitude for everything enhances this Love, unhappiness can't sneak in.

The Happiness Process

Consider again that happiness is our natural state. What if unhappiness is nothing more than unresolved energy 'blocking' our access to an inherent and natural state of happiness? Wouldn't an 'unblocking' be of great value?

Of course, a complete and permanent unblocking might take quite a while to complete. I have dedicated the last thirty-plus years of my life to developing techniques to rapidly accelerate this unblocking, also known as 'clearing.' Let's explore a possible brief clearing of happiness-blocking energy.

1. Let's imagine that we have a part of ourselves called the Holder-of-Unhappiness.

   a) He or she has reasons for resistance to happiness. It is very likely that this part is contracted and defensive.

2. Let's also imagine this less-bright or dimmer part of ourselves is just a small part, a sub-personality, not our entire personality.

3. Let's conceive of another part of ourselves, a safe, happy, unharmable part of ourselves, called the Holder-of-Happiness.

4. To help us feel safer, in this part, let's imagine this is a larger, brighter part of ourselves that exists as a light body. Still just a part, not our entire personality, but radiant.

5. Continue to dwell on this light body (being made of the luminous, it is unharmable, free, and totally capable of slipping beyond resistance).

   a) Think of this part of you as an aspect of your untethered or expanded Soul if that helps you envision and connect with it.

6. Stay with this warm, welcoming energy for a few minutes and then let it expand.

7. Gently bring back to mind the more fearful, resentful feelings lodged in the Holder-of-Unhappiness.

   a) Remember, there is nothing wrong or bad about these feelings.

   b) Remember, these blocking feelings can be honored and brought to Light.

8. Without making these darker emotions wrong or bad, imagine that you can surround them with compassionate awareness.

9. Create a safe space within which you can feel them safely, not trying to change them.

10. For a couple of minutes, continue to surround them with compassion.

11. After a couple of minutes, you may notice that the intensity in the darker emotions has diminished.

12. If you feel stuck or need a little more help and have an open mind to the presence of angels and supportive luminous beings, try asking, "Angels and luminous beings, I need some help. Please help me hold these darker emotions in Love so that they

can heal and evaporate, and my natural state of happiness can shine forth."

13. Say "thank you" if you feel you have been supported.

Quotes About How To Experience Happiness

"Knowing how to suffer well is essential to realizing true happiness."

~Thich Nhat Hanh

"In order for happiness to be extended and renewed, you have to learn how to feed your happiness."

~Thich Nhat Hanh

"Don't underestimate the value of Doing Nothing, of just going along, listening to all things you can't hear, and not bothering."

~A.A. Milne

"True happiness...is not attained through self-gratification, but through fidelity to a worthy purpose."

~Helen Keller

"If you find serenity and happiness, some may be jealous. Be happy anyway."

~Mother Teresa

"The happiness we discover in life is not about possessing or owning or even understanding. Instead, it is the discovery of this capacity to love, to have a loving, free, and wise relationship with all of life."

~Jack Kornfield

"Learn to let go. That is the key to happiness."

~Buddha

"I believe compassion to be one of the few things we can practice that will bring immediate and long-term happiness to our lives."

~H.H. Dalai Lama

"Happiness consists of living each day as if it were the first day of your honeymoon and the last day of your vacation."

~Leo Tolstoy

Happiness in the Four Stages of Life

We could look at life as having four major stages. According to Dr. S. Chandra, Indian philosophy describes these four stages as: Student, Householder, Retired, and Renunciate.

From a more western and psychological perspective, I suggest the following four stages: Childhood, Householder, Retired and Spiritually-focused. In all four stages, we find genuine happiness through experiences that create an awareness of a positive inner state. This can be expressed as an "I am" awareness.

Happiness in childhood can be found in loving connections, first with mother, then father and other family members. A child's happiness can be expressed in play, learning, and growth within a safe environment. A child might experience the inner state of happiness as an awareness of "I am safe," "I am Loved," "I am cared for."

Happiness as a householder can be experienced in relationships, accomplishments, activities, creating and supporting an attractive and safe environment. But for genuine happiness, outer achievement needs to correlate with self-awareness. "I am capable," "I am a good person," "I deserve to be happy," "I am enough."

If there is not an inner correlation, the result may well be cognitive dissonance. And when, through cognitive dissonance, the inner and outer are not in alignment, we usually change the inner or the outer to match. The result of which is, most often, the loss of happiness.

In retirement, happiness can be found in new freedoms, new opportunities, and the unfoldment of new and unused parts of ourselves. It is crucial for many in retirement to feel that they have a purpose, and reveal new parts of themselves. To be happy in retirement, we need to experience "I am contributing," "I am valuable," "I am Loved," "I am growing."

In the fourth stage, our spiritual growth and experience take center stage. While spiritual interests may well have been there all along, this stage invites a new depth of intent, devotion, and willingness to let go of attachment to aspects of the previous three stages.

We may direct these spiritual interests to God or our inner nature. Or, we may find immersion in nature, animals or a group effort.

Profound happiness exists in devotion to something greater than ourselves. In this, we can discover, "I am more than a limited self," "I am a part of something greater than myself," "I am One with my Father," "I am Loved by Divine Mother," "I am That."

Although we can describe our lives in four stages, there is a consistent reality to the experience of genuine happiness throughout our lives. This comes from being connected to our Best Self, and holding a positive sense of ourselves. This positive sense of ourselves allows us to internalize a positive, external experience as happiness.

The single contradiction to this is the awareness of our Self and The Self as One. This is always the highest form of happiness.

An Integration

Happiness is something we are. Pleasure is something we get. Excitement is something we can experience. Satisfaction is something we can achieve. Happiness, real happiness, is a state of Being.

It is not happiness if it is because of something external. If it is real happiness, then it is an awareness of the Soul's interconnectedness with All-That-Is.

"Out beyond ideas of wrongdoing and rightdoing there is a field," writes Rumi, "I'll meet you there."

True happiness is beyond our thinking minds. Just slip into Being, for It's there that happiness lies waiting.

Be willing, even for a moment, to let go, to own nothing – not even an identity.

When it is needed, it will be waiting when you emerge. And, when you do emerge from this loving field, you will know beyond a shadow of a doubt that it is a loving and benevolent universe.

And you will be happy.

In Essence

There are two kinds of happiness. There is the temporary happiness we get when something good happens to us.

We could call this "happeningness."

And then there is a sense of Wholeness, Love, Peace, and Divine Connection.

When any of these Soul-generated experiences occur, we feel Genuine Happiness because we know our Divine identity at that moment.

Chapter 14

INNER STILLNESS

The Peace That Passes Understanding

I nner Stillness is not a sensory experience. It is a state of consciousness. Silence and Peace can serve as doorways through which we can experience this Inner Stillness, and the Reality of our own True and inherent nature.

Many writers regard Silence and Stillness as being equal states, and their quotes reflect that. For clarity's sake, in this chapter, we will consider Inner Stillness to be the state of 'Immersion in Self' and identical with the Peace that goes beyond the mind.

We will explore silence and peacefulness as doorways to transcendent awareness, as pathways to Inner Stillness. Stillness is not the absence of noise. It is the result of a focus on what is non-changing. It is the result of immersion in the Self.

Why are Stillness, Silence and Peace so valued by those who live beyond the ego? The intellect is a limited, closed system. It is finite. It cannot comprehend infinity. It functions analytically to take things apart.

Stillness, being a peace that goes beyond our human understanding, exists beyond the intellect. Stillness can be experienced as a state of consciousness, an awareness that is indescribable, beyond words. As a beginner's mind holds more possibilities than the educated mind of ego, Stillness holds infinite possibilities.

Silence can be an essential pathway to Stillness. Entering into silence requires a determination to not be distracted, and to let the world go and follow an inward path. Then, to lovingly embrace and accept any thoughts or emotions that are activated by the inward dive. This acceptance offers the mind the possibility to grow quiet and move towards Stillness.

Questions for Self-Inquiry

- Does Stillness or silence have a negative connotation, or appear as frightening?

- Have you experienced Inner Stillness, but perceived it as empty?

- Do you believe that Inner Stillness is unavailable for most people?

- If you have experienced Inner Stillness, what would you be willing to let go of to experience it more fully?

The Value of Stillness and Silence

Sink into the quotes as if they were the ocean…not knowing what you're going to find….waiting for a meaning to reveal itself to you….as perhaps a feeling or a thought. You may feel complete after the experience of even one quote. (As a friend said, after feeling the

Stillness, "I felt fulfilled and somehow knew God is real. And I didn't want anything more at the moment I felt so full".)

Quotes About Stillness and Silence

"To meet everything and everyone through stillness instead of mental noise is the greatest gift you can offer the universe."

~Eckhart Tolle

"When you are willing to stop looking for something in thought, you find everything in silence."

~Gangaji

"I think 99 times and find nothing. I stop thinking, swim in silence, and the truth comes to me."

~Albert Einstein

"There is nothing in all creation so like God as stillness."

~Meister Eckhart

"It is only when you are in habitual distraction, lost in the illusion of my absence, that I cannot find you. I am breathing your body, thinking what are called your thoughts. I am the perceiver and the objects perceived. It is just a question of receiving me. Be still and receive me."

~Devaji

"Be still and know that I am God."

~Psalm 46:10 *(The Bible, New International Version)*

"For God alone, O my soul, wait in silence, for my hope is from Him."

~Psalm 62:5 *(The Bible, English Standard Version)*

You might like to experience this quote in the following way: Open to that part of you that desires God alone. This part of you is not your ego that thinks it desires God, but actually resists the experience of God, because it feels like the ego's undoing. Wait in Silence, letting all thought go, and returning to Silence after thought goes. Knowing that all it desires come from God, and God alone.

"We need Silence, just as much as we need air..."

~Thich Nhat Hanh

"Silence is something that comes from your heart, not from outside...The practice is how to find Silence in all the activities you do."

~Thich Nhat Hanh

Silence is used as a state of Being, a state of consciousness that we can relate to through the idea of the heart - a state of feeling and not thinking. As we grow and integrate this truth, we can begin to experience a witness - an observer state of consciousness.

Cosmic Silence is a plane of consciousness that cannot be expressed in words."

~Ram Dass

"How will you ever find peace unless you yield to love"

~Rabia al Basri

"Sitting still is a way of falling in love with the world and everything in it."

~Pico Iyer

"When we speak of Silence...It is a feeling in the heart of what is silent, unchanging: the common ground, which has always been with you...It is through this Silence that God speaks."

~Devaji

"Truth can be communicated only in silence."

~Bhagwan Shree Rajneesh

"When the human mind is calm and quiet, like the North Star, not shifting, the spirit is most open and aware. For one who sees this, the celestial Tao is within oneself."

~Li Daoqun *(Translated by Thomas Cleary)*

"I felt in need of a great pilgrimage so I sat still for three days and God came to me."

~Kabir

"To the mind that is still, the whole universe surrenders...Be still - Stillness reveals the secrets of eternity."

~Lao Tzu

"All that moves exhausts itself eventually. Only that which is still is for always."

~Sadghuru

Stillness Process: Why Does Part of Me Resist Stillness?

1. Sit with your eyes closed, and ask yourself, "Is there a part of me that wants to avoid this exercise...to avoid the experience of Stillness?"

2. Write down as many thoughts of resistance as you can.

   a) These might include: This is boring. I hate the feeling of being alone. This feels like punishment. I'm going to miss something important. I'm starting to feel panicky. I feel so alone. It makes me anxious – not checking my phone. I'm not good at this. I'm supposed to be doing something.

3. Finding the part of you we have called the Best Self, the caring, loving, non-judgmental part of you, speak to your resistance and say something like, "Of course you feel the way you do. It's totally understandable. And I'll stay here with you while you feel what you feel. You are not alone."

4. While this resistant part is receiving some positive attention, imagine that you are on a beach chair, by the ocean, or under an umbrella and let healing warmth support and nurture you.

5. After a short time (maybe around 2 minutes), let go of the visualization and spend a short time just feeling the Stillness. With practice and attention to the resistant parts, this period of Stillness can grow and deepen. And the resistance can turn into an embrace.

Stillness As a Path

There is perhaps no better insight into the pathlike nature of Stillness than as expressed by the Psalmist who wrote, "Be still and know that I am God." In Stillness we can step away from our egos, our cravings and our mindset. In Stillness, our Soul can reveal Itself. And yet, our egos resist Stillness, and even silence as if it were death. In some ways, it is. Stillness diminishes the ego. It is powerless there. Stillness, which is beyond the changing world, is our true Home, but not our ego's.

Quotes About Stillness As a Path

"All that is needed to realize the Self is to be still."

~Sri Ramana Maharshi

"It is not the outer form that changes; it is the nature of the inner being that fills the form. If you're a lawyer you go on being a lawyer, but you begin to use being a lawyer as a way of coming to God. One form is no more spiritual than any other. The essential work of developing a spiritual consciousness is quieting the mind and opening the heart."

~Ram Dass

"A soul that does not attain to a degree of purity corresponding to its capacity, will never find true peace."

~St. John of the Cross

"When you try to stop activity to achieve quietude your very effort fills you with activity…When the mind exists undisturbed in the Way there is no objection to anything in the world, and when there is no objection to anything, things cease to be – in the old way."

~Seng-ts'an

"In the midst of movement and chaos, keep stillness inside of you."

~Deepak Chopra

"Within yourself is a stillness, a sanctuary to which you can retreat at any time and be yourself."

~Hermann Hesse

"Yoga means stillness of mind and freedom from oscillations and various mental processes."

~Patanjali

"So the darkness shall be the light, and the stillness the dancing."

~T.S. Eliot

"Be the silent watcher of your thoughts and behavior. You are beneath the thinker. You are the stillness beneath the mental noise."

~Eckhart Tolle

"Stillness is where creativity and solutions to problems are found…It is the stillness that will save and transform the world."

~Eckhart Tolle

"Stillness is the only thing in this world that has no form. But then, it is not really a thing, and it is not of this world."

~Eckhart Tolle

"Just come into stillness. Have your intention be to relax with the breath. That will begin to set in motion a habit that will start to train the mind."

~Tara Brach

"Yet feeling emotional upheaval is not a spiritual faux pas; it is the place where the warrior learns compassion…It is only when we can dwell in these places that scare us that equanimity becomes unshakable."

~Pema Chödrön

A Process: One Way To Be With Emotional Upheaval

For many of us who perceive ourselves on a spiritual path, emotional difficulty and overwhelm can seem very frightening. Aren't we supposed to be feeling less and less attached, and more and more beyond such things?

There will be times in our journey when the deeper stresses and repressed traumas may come to consciousness. Our innate wisdom has perceived that possibly, now is the time for deep healing and greater Self-realization.

What has been growing within us all along is the awareness of the Witness Self, the observer.

While egoic healing is occurring, the Witness Self is becoming more available.

Let's invite the Witness Self Into Awareness:

1. Imagine a circle drawn on the ground.

2. Imagine it to be a puddle of emotional upheaval.

3. Spend a couple of minutes focusing entirely on the upheaval. This upset resides in your ego in the midst of a challenge.

4. Imagine an unattached, unafraid, unharmable, at peace part of your Self standing outside the circle…Just observing.

5. Acknowledge that the part of your ego involved with emotionally challenging experience is not the entirety of your Self.

6. Acknowledge that you are more than just your ego.

7. Recognize that you can be aware of both parts of yourself, perhaps even at the same time.

8. Remember, Awakening is in process.

An Integration

Beyond our fears, beyond all activity, there is Stillness-Silence-Peace.

It has to defend itself from nothing, for nothing can harm it.

It is so far beyond harm that the thought of harm is actually unthinkable.

Even though it is empty, at the same time, it is unimaginably full.

When it is lively within us, it is the Witness.

It enters not at all, and yet its very presence is Grace and brings a sense of wellbeing to conscious awareness.

It can be experienced as a fuller word than Love, and some know Stillness as the closest word to God.

In Essence

Stillness, Inner Silence and Peace are what we work towards but cannot achieve.

They are aspects of our True and Divine nature and therefore already exist within us.

They wait to be revealed and uncovered.

The ego casts a fearful shadow over them, hoping that it will feel safer if it is in control.

But, since we are so much more than our ego, the shadow of fear diminishes, and we come to know ourselves in Stillness and Peace.

Chapter 15

GRACE AND BLESSINGS

Divine Grace and Human Blessings

Grace is something that is divinely given. It blesses us. We cannot earn it. But, what we can learn is how to receive it, how to be Grace-ready. As Sri Sri Ravi Shankar once said, you cannot earn Grace, but you can learn how to hold your spoon hollow side up.

Could it be that all we receive from God comes through Grace, that God continually blesses us, yet we don't receive all that is given?

If we were always Grace-ready, then our lives would be joyful and one with all that is. We would be at peace with everything and everyone. All creation would be experienced as a blessing.

While it may be easy to imagine that God's Love is a direct expression of Grace, in this chapter, we'll explore the idea that people, animals and things of this world can also bless. When earthly things communicate God's Love, they bless. A Blessing is Grace with an earthly messenger.

Question for Self-Inquiry

- Could you be at peace with freely given and unearned Grace?
- Is it possible that life is constantly Blessing us?
- Do you fear losing your sense of self through the experience of Grace?
- Is it possible that Grace and Blessings are Love in action?

Grace

We can understand Grace as a divine expression of God's Love for creation. I believe that this Love is non-exclusive. Everyone and everything is included. God's Love is permanent, unchanging and always given.

We do not experience this constant Grace because we hide from it, or have egoic ideas about what Grace should look like and believe we are unworthy. In other words, all is given, but not all is received.

We also can find Grace in ourselves if we think from a perspective akin to Buddhism, and do not include God in our understanding. The innermost nature of our Best Self is a fountain of boundless blessings.

The legendary poet Kabir, summarizes the mystical perspective of the universality of God's Love and Grace in this poem, translated by Daniel Ladinsky.

"What kind of God would He be

If a leaf's prayer was not as precious to Creation

As the prayer His own son sang

From the glorious depth

Of his soul –

For us."

Love considers us Home when we live in a universe filled with Grace we live with a sense of safety and peace.

Quotes About Grace

"To be grateful is to recognize the Love of God in everything He has given us - and He has given us everything. Every breath we draw is a gift of His love, every moment of existence is a grace, for it brings with it immense graces from Him."

~Thomas Merton

"What would seem to need a thousand years can be done in a second by the grace of God."

~A Course in Miracles

"It is all for the best."

~Talmud, Ta'anit

"The Grace of God is dangerous. It's lavish, excessive, outrageous, and scandalous. God's Grace is ridiculously inclusive. Apparently God doesn't care who He loves."

~Mike Yaconelli

When you are spiritually connected...You are in a state of Grace in which you know you are connected to God and thus free from the effects of anyone or anything external to yourself."

~Wayne Dyer

"I'm becoming more and more myself with time. I guess that's what Grace is. The refinement of your Soul through time."

~Jewel

"The world is not imperfect or slowly evolving along a path to perfection. No, it is perfect at every moment, every sin already carries grace with it."

~Hermann Hesse

"I do not understand the mystery of Grace - only that it meets us where we are but does not leave us where it found us."

~Anne Lamott

"You are a volume in the divine book

A mirror to the power that created the universe

Whatever you want, ask it of yourself

Whatever you are looking for can only be found inside of you."

~Rumi

"It is not the law of religion nor the principles of morality that define our highways and pathways to God; only by the Grace of God are we led and drawn, to God. It is His Grace that conquers a multiple of flaws and in that Grace, there is only favor. Favor is not achieved; favor is received."

~C. JoyBell C.

Grace is the voice that calls us to change and then gives us the power to pull it off."

~Max Lucado

"Grace is God as heart surgeon, cracking open your chest, removing your heart – poisoned as it is with pride and pain – and replacing it with his own."

~Max Lucado

"Grace is not part of consciousness; it is the amount of light in our souls, not knowledge or reason."

~Pope Francis

"To live by Grace means to acknowledge my whole life story, the light side and the dark. In admitting my shadow side I learn who I am and what God's grace means."

~Brennan Manning

"Above all the grace and gifts that Christ gives to his beloved is that of overcoming self."

~St. Francis of Assisi

"If you depend on God's grace there is no such thing as impossible."

~Sri Chinmoy

Becoming Grace-Ready

What can we do to become Grace-ready if God is offering us Everything and we are not receiving this Gift? What can we do to hold our spoon right-side-up and expand the size of our spoon?

Belief is a key to receptivity. Jesus constantly spoke of the importance of belief, "…as thou hast believed, *so* be it done unto thee." *(Matthew 8:13 KJV)*.

If we believe that we are unworthy and undeserving, then our beliefs limit the goodness we can accept. Our sense of worthiness is changeable. Often, negative self-assessments result from painful childhood experiences that we haven't fully dealt with. These patterns and negative beliefs are healable *(See Chapter 3: Healing the Child Within)*

Teacher Thich Nhat Hanh offers a Buddhist approach. He's written: "The first of the Three Gems is the Buddha. When we say, "I take refuge in the Buddha" we should also understand that "The Buddha takes refuge in me," because without the second part the first part is not complete. The Buddha needs us for awakening, understanding, and love to be real things and not just concepts. They must be real things that have real effects on life. Whenever I say, "I take refuge in the Buddha," I hear "Buddha takes refuge in me."

Acceptance is another key to receptivity. Accepting whatever is happening now as a gift from God, and is perfect, allows us to learn from it, grow in it, and infuse the next moment with Love and insight.

From the Jewish perspective, Rebbe Menachem Schneerson has said, "There is no person, no thing, no scheme upon which your livelihood or your fate rests. There is only the flow of blessings from Above."

He instructs us to "Grasp the Source of Life"; and, we do this grasping by accepting that everything that exists in our world is about connecting us to the Creator. In other words, everything is Grace.

Gratitude is one of our greatest allies in opening to Grace. Gratitude opens our hearts when we have a spiritual, religious, or humanistic perspective. An open heart is receptive.

Harvard Medical School acknowledges the power of Gratitude. "Gratitude helps people feel more positive emotions, relish good experiences, improve their health, deal with adversity and build strong relationships." *(Cited in the Westwind Journal: "How To Start a Non-Religious Grace Practice").*

Gratitude for all challenges is a powerful spiritual practice that helps us circumvent our egos. Our egos always have a vested interest in the events of our lives. Our egos want to assess whether or not something benefits us directly.

We are functioning far beyond our egos when we can genuinely embrace Gratitude for all. And our higher Self, our Soul, is the part of our Self most Divinely connected. From this Divine connection, we can embrace everything.

Devotion is also a powerful tool to keep our spoon hollow-side up. By maintaining a committed, and ongoing spiritual focus, we can be open to Grace, whereas in an egoic state of self-absorption, we may completely ignore Grace's presence.

Devotion has a way of building up within us. Even a little devotion is far better than none. And, as Ramana Maharshi said, "If you wait till other desires disappear...you will have to wait for a very long time indeed." He adds that doubts never end, so don't let them distract you from devotion now.

Overcoming Fear is a key to allowing Grace to touch us. If we live in fear and survival, we will resist letting in something greater and more powerful than our ego. Supporting our fears with Love allows them to exist while Grace grows within us.

We are Blessed by the poet Hafez with the thought that if the rose didn't feel the encouragement of Light against its being, it would have remained too frightened to open its heart.

Be a Blessing Giver. A Blessing giver is someone who can let God shine through them. To the extent that we can be a channel of Divine Blessings, we, ourselves, are thusly Blessed. It is a spiritual principle that every gift we give from Spirit is also a gift to ourselves.

Blessings

Grace from God infuses us with holiness, and reminds us of our connection to Divine Love. God is not the only source of Blessing. We are blessed when anything that God creates communicates God's Love to us.

Blessings are gifts that allow us to freshly see from a greater distance. Blessings aren't just information; they are communications that make us more present and aware.

We are Blessed when we are in nature and experience the awe, wonder and beauty of creation. and when we share Love with the animals in our lives.

A Blessing may be guidance to take to heart, such as a warning that wakes you from past attachments. You may be Blessed by anger that makes you reconsider, or sweetness that melts your heart.

A Blessing may be a betrayal or rejection from a "friend" that reveals your neediness and codependency which can lead you to realize your courage and self-worth. A blessing can be rudeness that awakens a desire to act in a more loving way.

Most often, we experience a Blessing as an unexpected kindness and support that makes our lives better. A Blessing is Grace from an earthly messenger.

Quotes About Blessings

"The thing to do, it seems to me, is to prepare yourself so you can be a rainbow in someone else's cloud."

~Maya Angelou

"Some wish blessings, others pray for them. Some send blessings and they become one."

~Joyce C. Lock

"Vulnerable we are, like an infant. We need each other's care or we will suffer."

~St. Catherine of Siena *(Translated by Daniel Ladinsky)*

"When I started counting my blessings, my whole life turned around."

~Willie Nelson

"In the end, only three things matter: how much you loved, how gently you lived, and how gracefully you let go of things not meant for you."

~Buddha

"What seems to be bitter trials are often blessings in disguise."

~Oscar Wilde

"Being blessed is a condition of the heart and a frame of mind."

~Errin Rhorie

"Not being beautiful was the true blessing. Not being beautiful forced me to develop my inner resources. The pretty girl has a handicap to overcome."

~Golda Meir

An Exploration of the Ego's Resistance to Receiving

Have you ever felt diminished by being given a gift? To our egos, the giver may appear superior, and we may feel inferior. Perhaps we may feel indebted to the giver. Receiving a gift may trigger unconscious pain regarding other gifts we have or have not received.

We can be open to receiving the Good, the Light, and the Love that is meant for us, and that are sent to us when we become aware of our fears, resistances and prejudices. Not being Grace-ready would be like forgetting our address.

Please complete and write down your responses to the following sentences from feelings of resistance, fear, resentment, hostility and trauma. You may want to respond to each sentence numerous times. Please be aware that some of your emotions may take a little while to come to conscious awareness.

1. Sometimes when I receive a gift, a part of me feels
   _____.

2. I feel _____ when I see others getting what they want, and it makes me_____.

3. When I think about what my parents gave me or didn't give me, I feel _____.

4. Because I have done _____ I feel that I am not deserving.

5. Because I feel unlovable, God couldn't give me
   _____.

After completing the first part of the Process, now imagine yourself standing in the most beautiful, natural setting you could conceive. It's a perfect sunny day and the beauty is deeply touching you.

As you stand in the sunlight, allow yourself to imagine that the sunlight is just like unconditional Love. It demands nothing and gives everything freely. It is the source of life.

Let the Light wash into you and through you, and let it flush out all the negativity that is ready, willing and able to go.

Now go back and respond to the above five questions.

You may experience different answers this time.

An Integration

What if there is only Love in the universe? What if the things that seem so unfair, unkind, and evil are products of our own, limited egoic perspective? What if everything we experience is essential steps of growth to become more and more Grace-ready? What if everything is Grace?

If we believed this, then instead of fighting against what is happening, we could embrace it, learn from it and grow in Love. And, the more we grow in Love, the more Love finds us. When Love finds us, this is Grace. When we Love, this is Blessing. And, as we Bless others, we Bless ourselves.

Thank you God,

Thank you for all that I receive,

For all that I am.

For everything is You, and everything is Grace.

In Essence

Grace is an emanation and expression of God's Love. As God's Love is infinite, so is God's Grace. If God's Grace is infinite and Love is unconditional, then we are receiving Grace in every moment, in everything and in every way.

If this is not our experience, then we may well be resisting Grace, perhaps the way we might resist Love. Becoming aware of any resistance can be the beginning of a life lived differently.

While God or Spirit is the source of Grace, when Love is delivered by people or through Nature, we may also have the experience of being Blessed, enlivened or healed.

Knowing that we, as humans, have an opportunity to Bless opens and expands our hearts and can change our lives.

And everything of a spiritual nature we give, we also give to ourselves.

Acknowledgements

There are so many people to thank for the courage, support, training, and wisdom shared that facilitated the completion of this project. However, there is one clear place to begin. This book would never have come into existence if I weren't able to stand aside and let Spirit write through me. When this Guidance is flowing, I feel a flow of words and Truth and beauty of expression that transcends my personality.

Firstly, I acknowledge my mother, Molla. She was an artist, a healer and was passionately interested in all things metaphysical and spiritual. She set me on my path.

I also want to thank my father, Herbert. He was successful in the world of advertising and entertainment. It was through him that I was able to explore that world before taking a spiritual path.

Twenty years as a teacher of Transcendental Meditation (TM) and a student of Maharishi Mahesh Yogi provided me with my earliest and most profound spiritual education. I also bow deeply to Shri Shri Ravi Shanker, Devaji, and Panache Desai, with whom I have studied and matured through the years.I am profoundly grateful to Dr. Bill Little. I assisted Dr. Bill as his minister of Prayer for 20 years at the Pacific Coast Church, which later became The Center for Spiritual Awakening. I learned so much from him.

Benjamin Blumenthal has been an enormous help in the creation of this book. He is personally responsible for creating the list of authors at the end of the book.

I am so grateful to my son Daniel for his insight and loving help.

My appreciation also goes to our Miami sangha for their unwavering support.

My special and profound thanks go to Sapphire Grace, my first editor and writing coach.

This book would never have been brought into being without the dedication, skill, perseverance of my literary midwife, Deb Black.

My greatest and overarching thanks go to my wife, Robin. Her brilliant insights, loving support at every turn, and unwavering encouragement have allowed me to complete this book.

Thank you Marc Kaminsky. Your sensitivity, insight, nurturing, appreciation, and encouragement have been heart-empowering and mind-opening.

No dedication or expression of gratitude would be nearly complete if it didn't include the list of spiritual teachers and masters that opened in me the thirst for wisdom and the experience of Transcendent Reality. This list includes but is not limited to Paramahansa Yogananda, Maharishi Mahesh Yogi, Shri Shri Ravi Shankar, Mātā Amritānandamayī Dev (Amma), Devaji and Panache Desai.

Several authors and luminous beings are also central to the spirit that brought me to this book. These include Paramahansa Yogananda, Ramakrishna, Carl Jung, the translations of Daniel Ladinsky, David Richo and the material called A Course in Miracles.

I would be remiss if I didn't acknowledge the many friends and colleagues who were willing to be readers of this undertaking.

Thank you all!

About the Author

Rick Moss completed a PhD in education from the University of Texas at Austin. His dissertation was on Education and the Growth of Consciousness.

He has been interested in things of a spiritual nature for most of his life.

Rick received a master's degree in interdisciplinary studies in the light of consciousness from Maharishi International University, and has taught Transcendental Meditation™.

In the mid-1980s, realizing that meditation alone wasn't enough, he developed a process to free the mind from retained emotions and limiting beliefs to more fully experience the Love, Light and God qualities that exist within our Divine nature.

In addition, Rick is a Minister of Religious Science, and served as the Minister of Prayer at what is now called The Center for Spiritual Awakening.

He is the author of the e-book, "Awakening to Our Greatness" and "The Light-Travelers Notebook", and has also created the 15 companion CDs that comprise the Pre-Cognitive Re-Education Series.

For over thirty years, Rick has worked internationally with clients offering workshops, seminars and training.

To learn more about Rick, visit his extensive hands-on website: https://essentialpathways.com/

A Biography of Quoted Persons

A Course in Miracles: A 1976 book by Helen Schucman whose underlying premise is that the greatest "miracle" is the act of simply gaining a full "awareness of love's presence" in one's own life. The book seeks to find correlations with and corrections for the Bible. The Workbook of the Course offers a correction to egoic thinking.

Adyashanti: Born Stephen Gray, he is an American spiritual teacher and author. He is the author of numerous books, CDs and DVDs and, together with his wife Mukti, is the founder of Open Gate Sangha, Inc., a nonprofit organization established in 1996 which supports and makes available his teachings.

The Aetherius Society: A new religious movement founded by George King in the mid-1950s as the result of what King claimed were contacts with extraterrestrial intelligences, to whom he referred as "Cosmic Masters".

Muhammad Ali: American professional boxer, activist, entertainer, poet and philanthropist. Born Cassius Clay, and nicknamed The Greatest, he is widely regarded as one of the most significant and celebrated sports figures of the 20th century, and is frequently ranked as the greatest heavyweight boxer of all time.

James Allen: British philosophical writer known for his inspirational books and poetry, and as a pioneer of the self-help movement. His best known work, "As a Man Thinketh", has been mass-produced since its publication in 1903. It has been a source of inspiration to motivational and self-help authors.

Amma: Indian Hindu spiritual leader, guru and humanitarian, who is revered as 'the hugging saint' by her followers.

Maya Angelou: American poet, memoirist, and civil rights activist. She published seven autobiographies, three books of essays, several books of poetry, and is credited with a list of plays, movies, and television shows spanning over 50 years. She received dozens of awards and more than 50 honorary degrees.

Aristotle: Greek philosopher and polymath during the Classical period in Ancient Greece. He was the founder of the Lyceum, the Peripatetic school of philosophy, and the Aristotelian tradition. His writings cover many subjects including physics, biology, zoology, metaphysics, logic, ethics, aesthetics, poetry, theater, music, rhetoric, psychology, linguistics, economics, politics, meteorology, geology and government. His philosophy has exerted a unique influence on almost every form of knowledge in the West and it continues to be a subject of contemporary philosophical discussion.

Saint Augustine: Augustine of Hippo, also known as Saint Augustine, was a theologian and philosopher of Berber origin and the bishop of Hippo Regius in Numidia, Roman North Africa.

Marcus Aurelius: Roman emperor from 161 to 180 and a Stoic philosopher. He was the last of the rulers known as the Five Good Emperors, and the last emperor of the Pax Romana, an age of relative peace and stability for the Roman Empire. He served as Roman consul in 140, 145, and 161.

Sri Aurobindo: Indian philosopher, yoga guru, maharishi, poet, and Indian nationalist. He was also a journalist, editing newspapers such as Bande Mataram.

Richard Bach: American writer widely known as the author of some of the 1970s' biggest sellers, including Jonathan Livingston Seagull and Illusions: The Adventures of a Reluctant Messiah. Bach has written numerous works of fiction, and also non-fiction flight-related titles.

Sai Baba: Sai Baba of Shirdi was an Indian spiritual master who is regarded by his devotees to be a manifestation of Sri Dattaguru and identified as a saint and a fakir. He was likely born around 1838 and was revered by both his Hindu and Muslim devotees during, as well as after, his lifetime.

Li Bai: Also known as Li Bo, courtesy name Taibai, art name Qinglian Jushi, was a Chinese poet acclaimed from his own day to the present as a genius and a romantic figure who took traditional poetic forms to new heights.

Rabia al Basri: Rābiʿa al-ʿAdawiyya al-Qaysiyya was an Arab Muslim saint and Sufi mystic. She is known in some parts of the world as Hazrat Bibi Rabia Basri, Rabia of Basra, Rabia Al Basri or simply Rabia Basri.

Martha Beck: American author, life coach, and speaker who specializes in helping individuals and groups achieve greater levels of personal and professional success.

Ruth Bell Graham: American Christian author, most well known as the wife of evangelist Billy Graham. In 1959, she published her first book, Our Christmas Story, an illustrated volume for children. She went on to write or co-write 13 other books, many of them works of poetry.

Rabbi Israel ben Eliezer: Known as the Baal Shem Tov or as the Besht, was a Jewish mystic and healer from Poland who is regarded as the founder of Hasidic Judaism. "Besht" is the acronym for Baal Shem Tov, which means "One with the Good Name" or "one with a good reputation".

Herbert Benson: American medical doctor, cardiologist, and founder of the Mind/Body Medical Institute at Massachusetts General Hospital in Boston. He was a professor of mind/body medicine at Harvard Medical School and director emeritus of the Benson-Henry Institute at MGH.

Toba Beta: SyFy writer from Indonesia. He works as an economist/practitioner in Indonesian financial industries and capital markets. He writes journals, novels, quotes and poems.

Steve Bhaeman: Author, humorist, and political and cultural commentator who's been writing and performing enlightening comedy as Swami Beyondananda for over 20 years

Ma Jaya Sati Bhagavati: Devotee of Hindu Guru Neem Karoli Baba. She founded Kashi Ashram in Sebastian, Florida. Jaya's interfaith teachings included a blend of philosophy from Hinduism, Judaism, Christianity, Buddhism, Islam and other religions.

Bodhidharma: A semi-legendary Buddhist monk who lived during the 5th or 6th century. He is traditionally credited as the transmitter of Buddhism to China, and regarded as its first Chinese patriarch. According to Chinese legend, he also began the physical training of the monks of Shaolin Monastery that led to the creation of Shaolin Kung Fu. He is known as Dámó in China and as Daruma in Japan. His name means "dharma of awakening (bodhi)" in Sanskrit.

Joan Borysenko: A distinguished pioneer in integrative medicine, Joan is one of the leading experts on stress, spirituality, and the mind/body connection.

Tara Brach: American psychologist, author, and proponent of Buddhist meditation. Her colleagues in the Vipassanā, or Insight meditation tradition include Jack Kornfield, Sharon Salzberg, and Joseph Goldstein.

John Bradshaw: American educator, counselor, motivational speaker, and author who hosted a number of PBS television programs on topics such as addiction, recovery, codependency, and spirituality.

Barbara Brennan: American author, spiritual healer, businesswoman and teacher working in the field of energy healing. In 2011, she was listed by the Watkins Review as one of the most spiritually influential persons in the world.

Casandra Brené Brown: is an American research professor, lecturer, author, and podcast host. Brown is known in particular for her research on shame, vulnerability, and leadership. A long-time researcher and academic, Brown became famous following a widely-viewed TED talk in 2010. Since then she has written six number-one New York Times bestselling books, hosts two podcasts and has filmed a lecture for Netflix.

Buddha: Also known as Gautama Buddha, Siddhattha Gotama or Siddhārtha Gautama or Shakyamuni), was a teacher, philosopher and spiritual leader who lived in ancient India, and is considered the founder of the world religion of Buddhism. He is revered by Buddhists as an enlightened being who rediscovered an ancient path to freedom from ignorance, craving and the cycle of rebirth and suffering. His teaching is based on his insight into the arising of suffering or dissatisfaction and its ending — the state called Nirvana. During his meditation, all of the answers he had been seeking became clear, and he achieved full awareness, thereby becoming Buddha.

Frederick Buechner: American writer, novelist, poet, autobiographer, essayist, preacher, and theologian. He is an ordained Presbyterian minister and the author of more than thirty published books.

George Burns: American comedian, actor, singer, and writer. He was one of the few entertainers whose career successfully spanned vaudeville, radio, film, and television. His arched eyebrow and cigar-smoke punctuation became familiar trademarks for over three-quarters of a century.

C. JoyBell C: Author of books of poetry and literature that delve mainly into the mysterious, the philosophical and the esoteric.

Lucia Capacchione: Italian-American psychologist, art therapist, former graphic designer and a writer who has written twenty-two books based on child therapy and self-help, including The Creative Journal and Recovery of Your Inner Child.

Dale Carnegie: American writer and lecturer, and the developer of courses in self-improvement, salesmanship, corporate training, public speaking, and interpersonal skills. Author of How to Win Friends and Influence People (1936), a bestseller that remains popular today. He also wrote How to Stop Worrying and Start Living (1948), Lincoln the Unknown (1932), and several other books. One of the core ideas in his books is that it is possible to change other people's behavior by changing one's behavior towards them.

Saint Catherine of Genoa: Italian Roman Catholic saint and mystic, admired for her work among the sick and the poor and remembered because of various writings describing both these actions and her mystical experiences.

Saint Catherine of Siena: A lay member of the Dominican Order, she was a mystic, activist, and author who had a great influence on Italian literature and the Catholic Church. Canonized in 1461, she is also a Doctor of the Church.

Carlos Castaneda: American writer. Starting with The Teachings of Don Juan in 1968, Castaneda wrote a series of books that purport to describe training in shamanism that he received under the tutelage of a Yaqui "Man of Knowledge" named Don Juan Matus.

Cicero: Marcus Tullius Cicero was a Roman statesman, lawyer, scholar, and philosopher. His extensive writings include treatises on rhetoric, philosophy and politics, and he is considered one of Rome's greatest orators and prose stylists.

G. K Chesterton: English writer, philosopher, lay theologian, and literary and art critic. He has been referred to as the "prince of paradox".

Swami Chetanananda: A spiritual teacher, author, and highly accomplished practitioner of kundalini meditation and tantric sadhana.

Sri Chinmoy: Born Chinmoy Kumar Ghose, he was an Indian spiritual leader who taught meditation in the West. A prolific author, artist, poet, and musician, he also held public events such as concerts and meditations on the theme of inner peace.

Pema Chödrön: American Tibetan Buddhist. She is an ordained nun, former acharya of Shambhala Buddhism and disciple of Chögyam Trungpa Rinpoche. Chödrön has written several dozen books and audiobooks.

Deepak Chopra: Indian-American author and alternative medicine advocate. A prominent figure in the New Age movement, his books and videos have made him one of the best-known and wealthiest figures in alternative medicine.

Winston Churchill: British statesman who served as Prime Minister of the United Kingdom from 1940 to 1945, during the Second World War, and again from 1951 to 1955. Best known for his wartime leadership as Prime Minister, Churchill was also a Sandhurst-educated soldier, a Nobel Prize-winning writer and historian, a prolific painter, and one of the longest-serving politicians in British history.

Andrew Cohen: Spiritual leader who states that "traditional" enlightenment is the realization of the transcendental aspect of God, and it often goes hand in hand with the realization that the world is an illusion. A fundamental aspect of Cohen's Evolutionary Enlightenment is the distinction between what he sees as two fundamental, yet opposing, aspects of the human psyche: the "ego" and the "authentic self".

Stephen Covey: American educator, author, businessman, and keynote speaker. His most popular book is The 7 Habits of Highly Effective People.

Paula D'Arcy: Author, retreat leader, speaker, playwright, and former psychotherapist. In 2001 she established the Red Bird Foundation, which supports the growth and spiritual development of those in need throughout the world.

Li Daoqun: Taoist Master whose teachings have been translated by author Thomas Cleary

Kabir Das: 15th-century Indian mystic poet and saint, whose writings influenced Hinduism's Bhakti movement and his verses are found in Sikhism's scripture Guru Granth Sahib. He is known for being critical of both organized religion and religions.

Baba Hari Dass: Born in Almora, near Nainital, Uttarakhand (formerly United Provinces of British India), India, Dass was a yoga master, a silent monk, a builder of temples, and a commentator of Indian scriptural tradition of Dharma and Moksha. He was classically trained in Ashtanga Yoga – Raja Yoga of Patanjali (the Yoga of Eight Limbs), as well as Kriya Yoga, Ayurveda, Samkhya, Tantra Yoga, Vedanta, and Sanskrit.

Ram Dass: Born Richard Alpert, he was an American spiritual teacher, psychologist, and author who received teachings of Ashtanga Yoga by Baba Hari Dass. In 1967, Alpert traveled to India and became a disciple of Hindu guru Neem Karoli Baba who provided spiritual teachings, and gave him the name Ram Dass, meaning "Servant of Ram". His best-selling 1971 book, *Be Here Now*, which has been described by multiple reviewers as "seminal", helped popularize Eastern spirituality and yoga in the West.

Laura Davis: Author of six non-fiction books, including The Courage to Heal: For Women Survivors of Child Sexual Abuse, The Courage to Heal Workbook, etc.

Anthony de Mello: Also known as Tony de Mello was an Indian Jesuit priest and psychotherapist. A spiritual teacher, writer, and public speaker, de Mello wrote several books on spirituality and hosted numerous spiritual retreats and conferences. He's known for introducing many people in the West to mindfulness-based practices he sometimes called "awareness prayer".

Pierre Teilhard de Chardin: French Jesuit priest, scientist, paleontologist, theologian, philosopher and teacher. He was Darwinian in outlook and the author of several influential theological and philosophical books. He took part in the discovery of Peking Man.

Panache Desai: Contemporary thought leader and author whose message of love and acceptance has drawn thousands of people from around the world to his seminars and workshops. Not aligned with any religious or spiritual tradition, he empowers people to free themselves of pain, suffering, sadness, and self-limiting beliefs.

Devaji: Enlightened spiritual teacher and author of the book Illuminated by Love.

Mātā Amritānandamayī (Amma) Devī: Indian Hindu spiritual leader, guru and humanitarian, who is revered as 'the hugging saint' by her followers.

Charles Dickens: English writer and social critic. He created some of the world's best-known fictional characters and is regarded by many as the greatest novelist of the Victorian era. His works enjoyed unprecedented popularity during his lifetime and, by the 20th century, critics and scholars had recognized him as a literary genius.

Fyodor Dostoyevsky: Russian novelist, short story writer, essayist, and journalist. Dostoevsky's literary works explore the human condition in the troubled political, social, and spiritual atmospheres of 19th-century Russia, and engage with a variety of philosophical and religious themes.

Wayne Dyer: American self-help and spiritual author and a motivational speaker. His first book, Your Erroneous Zones is one of the best-selling books of all time, with an estimated 100 million copies sold to date.

Meister Eckhart: German Catholic theologian, philosopher and mystic, born near Gotha in the Landgraviate of Thuringia in the 13th century Holy Roman Empire. He has acquired a status as a great mystic within contemporary popular spirituality.

Mary Baker Eddy: American religious leader and author who founded The Church of Christ, Scientist in New England in 1879.

Albert Einstein: German-born theoretical physicist, widely acknowledged to be one of the greatest physicists of all time. Einstein is best known for developing the theory of relativity, but he also made important contributions to the development of the theory of quantum mechanics.

T.S. Eliot: Born Thomas Stearns Eliot, he was a poet, essayist, publisher, playwright, literary critic and editor. Considered one of the 20th century's major poets, he is a central figure in English-language Modernist poetry.

Black Elk: Born Heȟáka Sápa, was a wičháša wakȟáŋ ("medicine man, holy man"), heyoka of the Oglala Lakota people and educator about his culture. Black Elk is best known for relating his religious views, visions, and events from his life to poet John Neihardt who published these in his book Black Elk Speaks in 1932. Near the end of his life, he recorded the seven sacred rites of the Sioux to ethnologist Joseph Epes Brown which were published in 1947 in the book The Sacred Pipe.

Ralph Waldo Emerson: American essayist, lecturer, philosopher, abolitionist and poet who led the transcendentalist movement of the mid-19th century.

Donald Epstein: Chiropractor, developer of Network Spinal Analysis and author. Epstein is the founder and developer of Network Spinal Analysis and Somato Respiratory Integration, both revolutionary methods of promoting enhanced well-being. He is also the developer of Reorganizational Healing.

Antoine de Saint-Exupéry French writer, poet, aristocrat, journalist and pioneering aviator. He became a laureate of several of France's highest literary awards and also won the United States National Book

Award. He is best remembered for his novella The Little Prince (Le Petit Prince) and for his lyrical aviation writings, including Wind, Sand and Stars and Night Flight.

Marilyn Ferguson: American author, editor and public speaker known for her 1980 book The Aquarian Conspiracy which is connected with the New Age Movement.

Charles Finney: American Presbyterian minister and leader in the Second Great Awakening in the United States. He has been called the "Father of Old Revivalism." In his beliefs and teachings Finney departed from traditional Reformed theology by teaching that people have free will to choose salvation.

Jonathan Safran Foer: American novelist. He is known for his novels Everything Is Illuminated, Extremely Loud & Incredibly Close, Here I Am, and for his non-fiction works Eating Animals and We Are the Weather: Saving the Planet Begins at Breakfast.

Matthew Fox: Spiritual theologian, an Episcopal priest and an activist for gender justice and eco-justice. He has written 37 books that have been translated into other languages over 70 times. Among them are Original Blessing, The Coming of the Cosmic Christ, A Spirituality Named Compassion, The Reinvention of Work, The Hidden Spirituality of Men, Christian Mystics and The Pope's War.

Pope Francis: Born Jorge Mario Bergoglio, Pope Francis is the head of the Catholic Church and sovereign of the Vatican City State. Francis is the first pope to be a member of the Society of Jesus, the first from the Americas.

Saint Francis of Assisi: Born Giovanni di Pietro di Bernardone, he was an Italian Catholic friar, deacon, and mystic. He founded the men's Order of Friars Minor, the women's Order of St. Clare, the Third Order of St. Francis and the Custody of the Holy Land. Francis is one of the most venerated religious figures in Christianity.

Mohandas Karamchand Gandhi: known as Mahatma Gandhi, was an Indian lawyer, anti-colonial nationalist and political ethicist who employed nonviolent resistance to lead the successful campaign for India's independence from British rule, and to later inspire movements for civil rights and freedom across the world.

Gangaji: American-born spiritual teacher and author. She holds that the truth of who you are is already free and at peace, which can be realized simply by ending one's search.

Elizabeth Gilbert: American journalist and author. She is best known for her 2006 memoir, Eat, Pray, Love, which has sold over 12 million copies and has been translated into over 30 languages. The book was also made into a film of the same name in 2010.

Joel S. Goldsmith: American spiritual author, teacher, spiritual healer, and modern-day mystic. He founded The Infinite Way movement.

Daniel Goleman: Author and science journalist. For twelve years, he wrote for The New York Times, reporting on the brain and behavioral sciences. His 1995 book Emotional Intelligence was on The New York Times Best Seller list for a year-and-a-half, a best-seller in many countries, and is in print worldwide in 40 languages. Goleman has written books on other topics including self-deception, creativity, transparency, meditation, social and emotional learning, ecoliteracy and the ecological crisis, and the Dalai Lama's vision for the future.

Saint Gregory of Nyssa: Was bishop of Nyssa from 372 to 376 and from 378 until his death. He is venerated as a saint in Roman Catholicism, Eastern Orthodoxy, Oriental Orthodoxy, Anglicanism, and Lutheranism.

Kelsang Gyatso: Buddhist monk, meditation teacher, scholar, and author. He is the founder and former spiritual director of the New Kadampa Tradition-International Kadampa Buddhist Union.

Thich Nhat Hanh: Vietnamese Thiền Buddhist monk, peace activist, and founder of the Plum Village Tradition, historically recognized as the main inspiration for engaged Buddhism. Nhất Hạnh was active in the peace and deep ecology movements, promoting nonviolent solutions to conflict and raising awareness of the interconnectedness of all elements in nature. He was the founder of the largest monastic order in the West.

Mary Hartzell: Child development specialist and parent educator.

Louise Hay: American motivational and self-help author and minister. Author of the enormously successful book, You Can Heal Your Life. She was the founder of Hay House.

Heathcliff: Fictional character from Emily Bronte's book "Wuthering Heights", he is often regarded as an archetype of the tortured antihero whose all-consuming rage, jealousy and anger destroy both him and those around him.

Heraclitus of Ephesus: was an Ancient Greek, pre-Socratic, Ionian philosopher and a native of the city of Ephesus, which was then part of the Persian Empire. His paradoxical philosophy and appreciation for wordplay and cryptic utterances has earned him the epithet The Obscure since antiquity.

Hermann Hesse: German-Swiss poet, novelist, and painter. His best-known works include Demian, Steppenwolf, Siddhartha, and The Glass Bead Game, each of which explores an individual's search for authenticity, self-knowledge and spirituality. In 1946, he received the Nobel Prize in Literature.

Ernest Holmes: American New Thought writer, teacher, and leader. He was the founder of a spiritual movement known as Religious Science, part of the greater New Thought movement, whose spiritual philosophy is known as "The Science of Mind".

Rachel Hope: Certified Body Code and Emotion Code practitioner and founder of Rachel Hope Healing. She helps people to heal core wounding that tends to keep replaying in life through repeating painful patterns.

Jonathan Lockwood Huie: Has directed the product planning and implementation of numerous advanced technology products, including software, microcomputers, and ultra high speed network semiconductors. For 30 years, Mr. Huie coordinated the most advanced technologies with the realities of venture economics and customer acceptance.

Saint Ignatius: Spanish Catholic priest and theologian, who, with Peter Faber and Francis Xavier, founded the religious order of the Society of Jesus, and became the first Superior General of the Society of Jesus, at Paris, in 1541.

Ilaiyaraaja: Indian film composer, conductor-arranger, singer and lyricist who works in the Indian film industry, predominantly in Tamil. He is known for integrating Indian folk music and traditional Indian instrumentation with western classical music technique

Isaiah: was the 8th-century BC Israelite prophet after whom the Book of Isaiah is named. Within the text of the book, Isaiah himself is referred to as "the prophet", but the exact relationship between the Book of Isaiah and the actual prophet Isaiah is complicated.

Kobayashi Issa: Japanese poet and lay Buddhist priest of the Jōdo Shinshū. He is known for his haiku poems and journals. He is better known as simply Issa, a pen name meaning Cup-of-tea. He is regarded as one of the four haiku masters in Japan, along with Bashō, Buson and Shiki — "the Great Four."

Pico Iyer: British-born essayist and novelist known for his travel writing. He is the author of numerous books on crossing cultures including Video Night in Kathmandu, The Lady and the Monk and The Global Soul.

William James: American philosopher, historian, and psychologist, and the first educator to offer a psychology course in the United States. James is considered to be a leading thinker of the late 19th century, one of the most influential philosophers of the United States, and the "Father of American psychology."

Gerald Jampolsky: Author of Forgiveness: The Greatest Healer of All, is an internationally recognized authority in the fields of psychiatry, health, business, and education. Jampolsky is a child and adult psychiatrist and an inspirational speaker.

Jesus: Also known as Jesus Christ, was a Jewish teacher and reformer of religion who has become the main and central figure of Christianity. Christians follow the example of Jesus, accept his words to be true, and worship him as the incarnation of God. He is one of the most famous, most recognized, and most influential persons in the world's history.

Jewel: Born Jewel Kilcher is an American singer-songwriter, musician, actress, author and philanthropist. Jewel formed a nonprofit organization called Higher Ground for Humanity with her mother and older brother. The organization's focus is education, sustainable improvements, and building alliances with like-minded organizations.

Saint John of the Cross: Venerated as a Saint, John of the Cross, was a Spanish Catholic priest, mystic, and a Carmelite friar of converso origin. He is a major figure of the Counter-Reformation in Spain, and he is one of the thirty-six Doctors of the Church. John of the Cross is known especially for his writings.

John the Apostle: Or, Saint John the Beloved was one of the Twelve Apostles of Jesus according to the New Testament. Generally listed as the youngest apostle, he was the son of Zebedee and Salome. His brother was James, who was another of the Twelve Apostles.

Mother Juliana of Norwich: English anchoress of the Middle Ages. Her writings, now known as Revelations of Divine Love, are the earliest surviving English language works by a woman.

Carl Jung: Born Karl Gustav Jung, he was a Swiss psychiatrist and psychoanalyst who founded analytical psychology. Jung's work has been influential in the fields of psychiatry, anthropology, archeology, literature, philosophy, psychology and religious studies.

John Keats: English poet who was prominent in the second generation of Romantic poets, with Lord Byron and Percy Bysshe Shelley. Although his poems had been published for only four years when he died of tuberculosis at the age of 25, his fame grew rapidly after his death.

Helen Keller: American author, disability rights advocate, political activist and lecturer. Born in West Tuscumbia, Alabama, she lost her sight and hearing after a bout of illness at the age of nineteen months.

Sally Kempton: Nationally recognized as a master meditation and tantric philosophy teacher. A former Vedic swami, she has been teaching for nearly 40 years and is known for her practical insights into spiritual life, and for her powerful transmissions of meditative states.

Rose Fitzgerald Kennedy: American philanthropist, socialite, and a member of the Kennedy family. She was deeply embedded in the "lace curtain" Irish Catholic community in Boston, where her father John F. Fitzgerald was mayor. Wife of businessman and investor Joseph P. Kennedy Sr., who was United States Ambassador to the United Kingdom, formally known as Ambassador to the Court of St. James's in the UK. Their nine children included President John F. Kennedy, Senator Robert F. Kennedy, and longtime Senator Ted Kennedy. In 1951 she was ennobled by Pope Pius XII, becoming the sixth American woman to be granted the rank of Papal countess.

Katherine Ketcham: Coauthor of 13 books, including the New York Times bestseller Broken: My Story of Addiction and Redemption by William Moyers and the bestselling classics Under the Influence with James Milam and The Spirituality of Imperfection with Ernest Kurtz.

Søren Kierkegaard: Danish theologian, philosopher, poet, social critic, and religious author who is widely considered to be the first existentialist philosopher.

Martin Luther King, Jr. American Baptist minister and activist who became the most visible spokesman and leader in the American civil rights movement from 1955 until his assassination in 1968.

Kamand Kojouri: An author, poet and speaker who promotes and encourages women's academic research. Her first poetry collection, The Eternal Dance: Love Poetry and Prose, was published in March 2018.

Jack Kornfield: American author and teacher in the Vipassana movement in American Theravada Buddhism. He trained as a Buddhist monk in Thailand, Burma and India, first as a student of the Thai forest master Ajahn Chah and Mahasi Sayadaw of Burma.

Jiddu Krishnamurti: Indian philosopher, speaker and writer. In his early life, he was groomed to be the new World Teacher, but later rejected this mantle and withdrew from the Theosophy organization behind it.

Elisabeth Kübler-Ross: Swiss-American psychiatrist, a pioneer in near-death studies, and author of the 1969 internationally best-selling book, On Death and Dying, where she first discussed her theory of the five stages of grief, also known as the "Kübler-Ross model".

Ernest Kurtz: Author of Shame and Guilt, and, with Katherine Ketcham, The Spirituality of Imperfection. Published articles and has lectured nationally and internationally on subjects related to the academic study of spirituality.

Dalai Lama: His Holiness, The 14th Dalai Lama, known as Gyalwa Rinpoche to the Tibetan people, is the current Dalai Lama, the highest spiritual leader of Tibet, and a retired political leader of the nation. His teachings are about peace of mind, holiness and love.

Anne Lamott: American novelist, non-fiction writer, progressive political activist, public speaker, and writing teacher. Lamott's writings, marked by their self-deprecating humor and openness, cover such subjects as alcoholism, single-motherhood, depression, and Christianity. Her nonfiction works are largely autobiographical.

Llewellyn Vaughan Lee: Sufi mystic and lineage successor in the Naqshbandiyya-Mujaddidiyya Sufi Order. He is an extensive lecturer and author of several books about Sufism, mysticism, dreamwork and spirituality.

Samuel Levenson: American humorist, writer, teacher, television host, and journalist. Levenson wrote the well-known poem Time Tested Beauty Tips for his grandchild, which has become falsely attributed to Audrey Hepburn. He wrote Everything But Money, the bestseller Sex and the Single Child, In One Era And Out The Other, You Can Say That Again, Sam!, and You Don't Have to be in Who's Who to Know What's What.

Stephen Levine: American poet, author and teacher best known for his work on death and dying. He is one of a generation of pioneering teachers who, along with Jack Kornfield, Joseph Goldstein and Sharon Salzberg, have made the teachings of Theravada Buddhism more widely available to students in the West.

Jacob Lieberman: Pioneer in the fields of light, vision and consciousness, and the author of Luminous Life: How The Science Of Light Unlocks The Art Of Living, Light: Medicine Of The Future, Take Off Your Glasses And See, and Wisdom From An Empty Mind. Originally trained as an optometrist and vision scientist, his life changed in 1976 after the miraculous healing of his own eyesight, leading him to a deeper understanding of light and the science of life.

Abraham Lincoln: American lawyer and statesman who served as the 16th president of the United States from 1861 until his assassination in 1865. Lincoln led the nation through the American Civil War and succeeded in preserving the Union, abolishing slavery, bolstering the federal government, and modernizing the U.S. economy.

Bruce Lipton: American developmental biologist notable for his views on epigenetics. In his book The Biology of Belief, he claims that beliefs control human biology rather than DNA and inheritance.

Joyce. C. Lock: Author, poet, and columnist.

Max Lucado: American author and minister.

Luke: Or, Luke the Evangelist was one of the Four Evangelists—the four traditionally ascribed authors of the canonical gospels. He is believed to have contributed over a quarter of the text of the New Testament, more than any other author.

Marlena S. Lyons: Author, therapist and workshop leader. Co-author of the book Undefended Love.

Sri Nisargadatta Maharaj: Born Maruti Shivrampant Kambli, he was an Indian guru of nondualism, belonging to the Inchagiri Sampradaya, a lineage of teachers from the Navnath Sampradaya and Lingayat Shaivism.

Ramana Maharshi: Indian Hindu sage and jivanmukta. He was born Venkataraman Iyer, but is mostly known by the name Bhagavan Sri Ramana Maharshi.

Nelson Mandela: South African anti-apartheid revolutionary, political leader and philanthropist. He was the country's first black head of state and the first elected in a fully representative democratic election.

Brennan Manning: Born Richard Francis Xavier Manning was an American author, laicized priest, and public speaker. He is best known for his bestselling book The Ragamuffin Gospel.

Gabor Maté: Hungarian-Canadian physician and author. He believes in the connection between mind and body health. He has authored four books exploring topics including ADHD, stress, developmental psychology, and addiction.

Henri Matisse: French artist, known for both his use of color and his fluid and original draftsmanship. He was a draftsman, printmaker, and sculptor, but is known primarily as a painter.

Matthew the Apostle: One of the twelve apostles of Jesus. According to Christian traditions, he was also one of the four Evangelists as author of the Gospel of Matthew, and thus is also known as Matthew the Evangelist.

W. Somerset Maugham: English playwright, novelist, and short-story writer. He was among the most popular writers of his era and reputedly the highest-paid author during the 1930s.

Golda Meir: Israeli politician, teacher, and kibbutznikit who served as the fourth prime minister of Israel. She was the first woman to become head of government in Israel.

Thomas Merton: American Trappist monk, writer, theologian, mystic, poet, social activist, and scholar of comparative religion. On May 26, 1949, he was ordained to the Catholic priesthood and given the name "Father Louis".

Alice Miller: Psychologist teacher and author whose poetry actively influenced political opinion during the American suffrage movement, and whose verse novel The White Cliffs influenced political thought during the U.S.'s entry into World War II. Prisoners of Childhood, The Drama of the Gifted Child and the Search for the True Self offer essential perspectives, illuminating the need for inner child healing.

Henry Miller: American writer and artist. He was known for breaking with existing literary forms and developing a new type of semi-autobiographical novel that blended character study, social criticism, philosophical reflection, stream of consciousness, explicit language, sex, surrealist free association, and mysticism.

A.A. Milne: English author, best known for his books about the teddy bear Winnie-the-Pooh and for various poems.

John Milton: English poet and intellectual who served as a civil servant for the Commonwealth of England under its Council of State and later under Oliver Cromwell. He wrote at a time of religious flux and political upheaval, and is best known for his epic poem Paradise Lost.

Mirabai: Hindu mystic poet and devotee of Krishna. She is a celebrated Bhakti saint, particularly in the North Indian Hindu tradition.

David Stephen Mitchell: English novelist who has published seven novels two of which, number9dream and Cloud Atlas, were shortlisted for the Booker Prize.

Marilyn Monroe: American actress, model and singer. Famous for playing comedic "blonde bombshell" characters, she became one of the most popular sex symbols of the 1950s and early 1960s and was emblematic of the era's sexual revolution. She was one of the first women to own her own production company.

Mooji: Jamaican-born spiritual teacher.

Thomas Moore: Irish writer, poet, and lyricist celebrated for his Irish Melodies. Their setting of English-language verse to old Irish tunes marked the transition in popular Irish culture from Irish to English.

James Morcan: Australian-New Zealand author of two bestselling novels, including The Ninth Orphan with his father Lance.

Toni Morrison: American novelist. Her first novel, The Bluest Eye was published in 1970. The critically acclaimed Song of Solomon brought her national attention and won the National Book Critics Circle Award.

Rick Moss: Completed a PhD in education from the University of Texas at Austin. His dissertation was on Education and the Growth of Consciousness. Rick received a master's degree in interdisciplinary studies in the light of consciousness from Maharishi International University, and has taught Transcendental Meditation™. He is the author of the e-book, Awakening to Our Greatness and The Light-Travelers Notebook.

Elijah Muhammad: American religious leader, black separatist, and self-proclaimed Messenger of Allah, who led the Nation of Islam (NOI) from 1934 until his death in 1975. Teacher and mentor of Malcolm X, Louis Farrakhan, Muhammad Ali, and his own son, Warith Deen Mohammed.

John Muir: Influential Scottish-American naturalist, author, environmental philosopher, botanist, zoologist, glaciologist, and early advocate for the preservation of wilderness in the United States of America.

Swami Muktananda: Yoga guru, the founder of Siddha Yoga. He was a disciple of Bhagavan Nityananda. He wrote books on the subjects of Kundalini Shakti, Vedanta, and Kashmir Shaivism, including a spiritual autobiography entitled The Play of Consciousness.

Jocelyn Murray: Author of the teen/young adult historical fiction series The Gilded Mirror.

Caroline Myss: American Author, speaker on medical intuitive, spirituality and mysticism. She is most well known for publishing Anatomy of the Spirit in 1996.

Gurū Nānak: also referred to as Bābā Nānak, was the founder of Sikhism and is the first of the ten Sikh Gurus. Nanak is said to have traveled far and wide across Asia teaching people the message of ik onkar (ੴ, 'one God'), who dwells in every one of his creations and constitutes the eternal Truth

Willie Nelson: American musician, actor, and activist, he is one of the most recognized artists in country music. He was one of the main figures of outlaw country, a subgenre of country music that developed in the late 1960s as a reaction to the conservative restrictions of the Nashville sound

Friedrich Nietzche: German philosopher, cultural critic and philologist whose work has exerted a profound influence on modern intellectual history. He began his career as a classical philologist before turning to philosophy.

Anaïs Nin: French-Cuban-American diarist, essayist, novelist. In addition to her journals and collections of erotica, Nin wrote several works of non-fiction.

Henri Nouwen: Dutch Catholic priest, professor, writer and theologian. His interests were rooted primarily in psychology, pastoral ministry, spirituality, social justice and community.

Barack Obama: 44th President, and the first African-American President of the United States.

Suze Orman: American financial advisor, author, and podcast host. In 1987, she founded the Suze Orman Financial Group. Her work as a financial advisor gained notability with The Suze Orman Show, which ran on CNBC from 2002 to 2015.

Dean Ornish: American physician and researcher, Ornish is known for his lifestyle-driven approach to the control of coronary artery disease (CAD) and other chronic diseases. He promotes lifestyle changes including quasi-whole foods, plant-based diet, smoking cessation, moderate exercise, stress management techniques including yoga and meditation, and psychosocial support.

Joel Osteen: American pastor, televangelist, and author, based in Houston, Texas.

Leroy "Satchel" Paige: American professional baseball pitcher who played in Negro league baseball and Major League Baseball. His career spanned five decades and culminated with his induction into the National Baseball Hall of Fame.

B.J. Palmer: American chiropractor, son of Daniel David Palmer, the founder of chiropractic. BJ Palmer became known as the "Developer" of chiropractic.

D.D. Palmer: Founder of Chiropractic. Palmer believed that the human body had an ample supply of natural healing power transmitted through the nervous system. He suggested that if any one organ was affected by an illness, it merely must not be receiving its normal "nerve supply" which he dubbed a "spinal misalignment", or subluxation. He saw chiropractic as a form of realigning to reestablish the supply.

Patanjali: Thought to be the author of a number of Sanskrit and Tamil works, he was a sage in ancient Tamilakam. The greatest of these are the Yoga Sutras, a classical yoga text.

Saint Patrick: Romano-British Christian missionary and bishop in Ireland. Known as the "Apostle of Ireland", he is the primary patron saint of Ireland, the other patron saints being Brigit of Kildare and Columba.

Sri Ramakrishna Paramahamsa: Indian Hindu mystic and religious leader in 19th-century Bengal.

Saint Paul: Commonly known as Paul the Apostle and Saint Paul, was a Christian apostle who spread the teachings of Jesus in the first-century world. He is generally regarded as one of the most important figures of the Apostolic Age, he founded several Christian communities in Asia Minor and Europe from the mid-30s to the mid-50s AD.

Alan Paton: South African author and anti-apartheid activist. His works include the novels Cry, the Beloved Country and Too Late the Phalarope.

M. Scott Peck: American psychiatrist and best-selling author who wrote the book The Road Less Traveled, published in 1978.

Candace Pert: American neuroscientist and pharmacologist who discovered the opiate receptor, the cellular binding site for endorphins in the brain. Known for opiate receptors, pioneer in mind-body medicine, and HIV treatment. Pert published over 250 scientific articles on peptides and their receptors and the role of these neuropeptides in the immune system. She held a number of patents for modified peptides in the treatment of psoriasis, Alzheimer's disease, chronic fatigue syndrome, stroke and head trauma.

Joseph Pilates: German physical trainer, credited with inventing and promoting a method of physical fitness. Pilates came to believe that the "modern" lifestyle, bad posture, and inefficient breathing lay at the roots of poor health. He ultimately devised a series of exercises and training techniques, and engineered all the equipment, specifications, and tuning required to teach his methods properly.

Peace Pilgrim: Born Mildred Lisette Norman, she was an American spiritual teacher, mystic, pacifist, vegetarian activist and peace activist. In 1952, she became the first woman to walk the entire length of the Appalachian Trail in one season.

Edgar Allan Poe: American writer, poet, editor, and literary critic. Poe is best known for his poetry and short stories, particularly his tales of mystery and the macabre. He is widely regarded as a central figure of Romanticism in the United States, and of American literature. Poe was one of the country's earliest practitioners of the short story, and considered to be the inventor of the detective fiction genre, as well as a significant contributor to the emerging genre of science fiction.

Marcel Proust: French novelist, critic, and essayist who wrote the monumental novel In Search of Lost Time, originally published in French in seven volumes between 1913 and 1927. He is considered by critics and writers to be one of the most influential authors of the 20th century.

Jett Psaris: Co-author of Undefended Love, a Nautilus Award finalist for distinguished contribution to conscious living and positive change. For the past 30 years Jett has been in private practice working with couples and individuals, and has facilitated small groups and led workshops in the U.S. and abroad.

Diana Raab: American author, poet, lecturer, educator and inspirational speaker. Her research involved the transformative and healing aspects of memoir writing.

Raj Raghunathan: Zale Centennial Professor of Business at the McCombs School of Business at The University of Texas at Austin. He is interested in exploring the impact that people's judgments and decisions have on their happiness and fulfillment. Raj's work juxtaposes theories from psychology, behavioral sciences, decision theory and marketing to document and explain interrelationships between affect and consumption behavior.

Ramakrishna: Indian Hindu mystic and religious leader in 19th-century Bengal.

Lissa Rankin: Mind-body medicine physician, and founder of the Whole Health Medicine Institute training program for physicians and other health care providers, and the New York Times bestselling author of Mind Over Medicine: Scientific Proof That You Can Heal Yourself.

Amit Ray: Indian author and "spiritual master". He is known for his teachings on meditation, yoga, peace and compassion. He is best known for his Om meditation and integrated yoga and vipassana meditation techniques. He is the author of several books on meditation and other spiritual topics. He was one of the pioneers in proposing compassionate artificial intelligence.

Richard Rhor: American Franciscan priest and writer on spirituality. PBS has called him "one of the most popular spirituality authors and speakers in the world".

Errin Rhorie: Speaker and author

David Richo: Psychotherapist, teacher, writer, and workshop leader whose work emphasizes the benefits of mindfulness and loving-kindness in personal growth and emotional well-being.

Sogyal Rinpoche: Born Sonam Gyaltsen Lakar, he was a Tibetan Dzogchen lama of the Nyingma tradition. He was recognized as the incarnation of a great Tibetan master and visionary saint of the nineteenth century, Tertön Sogyal Lerab Lingpa.

Dennis Rivers: Semi-nomadic writer/teacher/peace activist/systems analyst who for many years taught communication skills in association with the Santa Barbara Community Counseling Center.

Will Rogers: American stage and film actor, vaudeville performer, cowboy, humorist, newspaper columnist, and social commentator from Oklahoma. He was a Cherokee citizen born in the Cherokee Nation, Indian Territory.

Eleanor Roosevelt: First lady of the United States and wife to Franklin D Roosevelt, the 32nd President of the United States. She was a political figure, diplomat, and activist.

Emmy Rossum: American actress and singer also known for her charity work and advocacy.

Wilma Rudolph: American sprinter, who became a world-record-holding Olympic champion and international sports icon in track and field following her successes in the 1956 and 1960 Olympic Games.

Mewlana Jalaluddin Rumi: Also known as Jalāl ad-Dīn Mohammad Balkhī was a Persian poet, Hanafi faqih, Islamic scholar, Maturidi theologian, and Sufi mystic originally from Greater Khorasan in Greater Iran. Rumi's influence transcends national borders and ethnic divisions. His poems have been widely translated into many of the world's languages and transposed into various formats.

Oliver Sacks: British neurologist, naturalist, historian of science, and writer. His numerous other best-selling books were mostly collections of case studies of people, including himself, with neurological disorders. He also published hundreds of articles (both peer-reviewed scientific articles and articles for a general audience), not only about neurological disorders but also insightful book reviews and articles about the history of science, natural history, and nature.

Sadghuru: Indian yoga guru and proponent of spirituality. In 1992 he established the Isha Foundation near Coimbatore, which operates an ashram and yoga center that carry out educational activities.

George Sand: Amantine Lucile Aurore Dupin, best known by her pen name George Sand, was a French novelist, memoirist, and journalist.

Menachem Mendel Schneerson: Known to many as the Lubavitcher Rebbe or simply the Rebbe, was a Russian-Empire-born American Orthodox rabbi, and the most recent rebbe of the Lubavitch Hasidic dynasty. He is considered one of the most influential Jewish leaders of the 20th century.

Arnold Schwarzenegger: Austrian, naturalized American film actor, former bodybuilder, producer, businessman, and former politician who served as the 38th governor of California. The movie icon and former governor Arnold Schwarzenegger is recognized as a global leader in the fight against climate change. As Governor of California, he took significant steps to reduce the state's greenhouse gas emissions, fought for stricter fuel-efficiency standards, and initiated a network of hydrogen filling stations and a large-scale installation of solar panels.

Seng-ts'an: Born Jianzhi Sengcan, known as the Third Chinese Patriarch of Chán after Bodhidharma and thirtieth Patriarch after Siddhãrtha Gautama Buddha. He is considered to be the Dharma successor of the second Chinese Patriarch, Dazu Huike.

Tal Ben Shahar: American and Israeli teacher, and writer in the areas of positive psychology and leadership. As a lecturer at Harvard University, Ben-Shahar created the most popular course in Harvard's history and has authored several best-selling books.

William Shakespeare: English playwright, poet and actor, widely regarded as the greatest writer in the English language and the world's greatest dramatist. He is often called England's national poet and the "Bard of Avon".

Ravi Shankar: Indian sitarist and composer. A sitar virtuoso, he became the world's best-known exponent of North Indian classical music in the second half of the 20th century, and influenced many musicians in India and throughout the world.

Sri Sri Ravi Shankar: Indian guru, a spiritual leader. He is frequently referred to as "Sri Sri", Guruji, or Gurudev. In 1981, he founded the Art of Living Foundation.

George Bernard Shaw: At his insistence, he preferred to be known simply as Bernard Shaw. He was an Irish playwright, critic, polemicist and political activist. His influence on Western theater, culture and politics extended from the 1880s to his death and beyond.

Bhagwan Shree: Also known as Acharya Rajneesh, Bhagwan Shree Rajneesh, and later as Osho, he was an Indian mystic and founder of the Rajneesh movement. During his lifetime, he was viewed as a controversial new religious movement leader. He rejected institutional religions and emphasized the importance of freethought, meditation, mindfulness, love, celebration, courage, creativity, and humor— qualities that he viewed as being suppressed by adherence to static belief systems.

Daniel J. Siegel: Siegel is a clinical professor of psychiatry, and is founding co-director of the Mindful Awareness Research Center at UCLA. Siegel's 2010 book, Mindsight: The New Science of Personal Transformation offers an in-depth exploration of the power of the mind to integrate the brain and promote well-being. He has written five parenting books. Siegel's most recent work integrates the theories of Interpersonal Neurobiology with the theories of Mindfulness Practice and proposes that mindfulness practice is a highly developed process of both inter and intra personal attunement.

Angelus Silesius: Born Johann Scheffler, also known as Johann Angelus Silesius, was a 17th-century German Catholic priest and physician, known as a mystic and religious poet. Silesius's poetry directs the reader to seek a path toward a desired spiritual state, an eternal stillness, by eschewing material or physical needs and the human will.

Michael A. Singer: American author, journalist, motivational speaker, and former software developer. Two of his books, The Untethered Soul and The Surrender Experiment, were New York Times bestsellers.

Socrates: Greek philosopher from Athens who is credited as a founder of Western philosophy and the first moral philosopher of the ethical tradition of thought.

Nicholas Sparks: American novelist, screenwriter, and philanthropist. He has published twenty-two novels and two non-fiction books, all of which have been New York Times bestsellers, with over 115 million copies sold worldwide in more than 50 languages.

Ringo Starr: English musician, singer, songwriter, actor, and philanthropist, Ringo Starr (Richard Starkey) achieved international fame as the drummer for the Beatles, and later his own All Starr Band. With his wife, the actress Barbara Bach, he started The Lotus Foundation which funds, supports, participates in and promotes charitable projects aimed at advancing social welfare in diverse areas.

Gloria Steinem: American feminist journalist and social-political activist who became nationally recognized as a leader and a spokeswoman for the American feminist movement in the late 1960s and early 1970s. Steinem was a columnist for New York Magazine, and a co-founder of Ms. magazine.

Rudolf Steiner: Austrian philosopher, social reformer, architect, esotericist, and a claimed clairvoyant. Steiner gained initial recognition at the end of the nineteenth century as a literary critic and published philosophical works including The Philosophy of Freedom.

Shunryu Suzuki: Often called Suzuki Roshi, was a monk and teacher who helped popularize Zen Buddhism in the United States, and is renowned for founding the first Zen Buddhist monastery outside Asia.

J.A. Symonds: English poet and literary critic. A cultural historian, he was known for his work on the Renaissance, as well as numerous biographies of writers and artists.

Rabindranath Tagore: Indian polymath, poet, writer, playwright, composer, philosopher, social reformer and painter. He reshaped Bengali literature and music as well as Indian art with Contextual Modernism.

Ryōkan Taigu: A quiet and unconventional Sōtō Zen Buddhist monk who lived much of his life as a hermit. Ryōkan is remembered for his poetry and calligraphy, which present the essence of Zen life. He is also known by the name Ryokwan in English.

The Talmud: The central text of Rabbinic Judaism and the primary source of Jewish religious law and Jewish theology.

Cathryn Taylor: Licensed MFT and Addictions Counselor, author of multiple books on the inner child and multidimensional healing. She is certified as an EFT practitioner and Akashic Records Consultant.

Alfred Lord Tennyson: English Poet Laureate during much of Queen Victoria's reign, he remains one of the most popular British poets. A number of phrases from Tennyson's work have become commonplace in the English language, including "Tis better to have loved and lost Than never to have loved at all", "Theirs not to reason why, Theirs but to do and die", "My strength is as the strength of ten", "Because my heart is pure", and "Knowledge comes, but Wisdom lingers". He is the ninth most frequently quoted writer in The Oxford Dictionary of Quotations.

Mother Teresa: Albanian-Indian Roman Catholic nun and missionary. She is honored in the Catholic Church as Saint Teresa of Calcutta, who, in 1950, founded the Missionaries of Charity, a Catholic religious congregation that had over 4,500 nuns and was active in some 133 countries.

Saint Teresa of Ávila: Also called Saint Teresa of Jesus, was a Spanish noblewoman who was called to convent life in the Catholic Church. A Carmelite nun, prominent Spanish mystic, religious reformer, author, theologian of contemplative life and of mental prayer, she earned the rare distinction of being declared a Doctor of the Church, but not until over four centuries after her death.

Saint Thomas Aquinas: An Italian Dominican friar, he was a philosopher, Catholic priest, and Doctor of the Church. An immensely influential philosopher, theologian, and jurist in the tradition of scholasticism, he is also known within the latter as the Doctor Angelicus, the Doctor Communis, and the Doctor Universalis

Henry David Thoreau: American naturalist, essayist, poet, and philosopher. A leading transcendentalist, he is best known for his book Walden, a reflection upon simple living in natural surroundings, and his essay "Civil Disobedience", an argument for disobedience to an unjust state.

Eckhart Tolle: German-born spiritual teacher and self-help author who resides in Canada. He is best known as the author of the New York Times Bestsellers The Power of Now and, A New Earth: Awakening to Your Life's Purpose.

Leo Tolstoy: Russian writer who is regarded as one of the greatest authors of all time. He received nominations for the Nobel Prize in Literature every year from 1902 to 1906 and for the Nobel Peace Prize in 1901, 1902, and 1909. Tolstoy is best known for the novels War and Peace and Anna Karenina, which are often cited as pinnacles of realist fiction.

Chuang Tzu: was a philosopher in ancient China who believed that life is transitory, and that the pursuit of wealth and personal aggrandizement were vain follies, which distracted from seeing and understanding the world and contemplating its meaning. He strove to see nature with new eyes.

Lao Tzu: also called Laozi and Lao-Tze, was an ancient Chinese philosopher and writer. He is the reputed author of the Tao Te Ching, the founder of philosophical Taoism, and a deity in religious Taoism and traditional Chinese religions.

Chandogya Upanishad: A Sanskrit text embedded in the Chandogya Brahmana of the Sama Veda of Hinduism. It is one of the oldest Upanishads, and is notable for its lilting metric structure, its mention of ancient cultural elements such as musical instruments, and embedded philosophical premises that later served as the foundation for the Vedanta school of Hinduism.

Jeffrey Van Dyk: International speaker, strategist and guide who works with highly successful leaders and founders in the second half of life who know that they are meant to transition into their life's legacy and have a meaningful, lasting impact on the world.

Iyanla Vanzant: American inspirational speaker, lawyer, New Thought spiritual teacher, author, life coach, and television personality.

Doreen Virtue: Spiritual doctor of psychology and fourth-generation metaphysician working with angelic, elemental, and ascended-master realms in writings and workshops. She has authored books about angels, chakras, children, health, diet, and other mind-body-spirit issues, including the best-selling Healing with the Angels and Messages from Your Angels books/angel cards.

Paramahamsa Vishwananda: Swami Vishwananda is the founder of Bhakti Marga, a neo-Hindu organization that has ashrams and temples in many countries.

Swami Vivekananda: Indian Hindu monk and philosopher. He was a chief disciple of the 19th-century Indian mystic Ramakrishna.

Stephanie Bennett Vogt: A leading space clearing expert, teacher, and author of five books and four online courses, she brings forty years of teaching experience to SpaceClear, the practice she founded in 1996 to help homes and people come into balance.

B. Alan Wallace: American author and expert on Tibetan Buddhism. His books discuss Eastern and Western scientific, philosophical, and contemplative modes of inquiry, often focusing on the relationships between science and Buddhism. He is the founder of the Santa Barbara Institute for Consciousness Studies.

Neal Donald Walsch: American author of the series Conversations with God. He is also an actor, screenwriter, and speaker.

Alan Watts: English writer, theologian, and speaker known for interpreting and popularizing Eastern philosophies such as Buddhism, Taoism, and Advaita Vedanta (Non-dualism) for a Western audience.

Walt Whitman: American poet, essayist and journalist. A humanist, he was a part of the transition between transcendentalism and realism, incorporating both views in his works. Whitman is among the most influential poets in the American canon, often called the father of free verse.

Ken Wilber: American philosopher and writer on transpersonal psychology and his own integral theory, a philosophy that suggests the synthesis of all human knowledge and experience.

Oscar Wilde: Irish poet and playwright. After writing in different forms throughout the 1880s, he became one of the most popular playwrights in London in the early 1890s. He is best remembered for his epigrams and plays, his novel The Picture of Dorian Gray

Thornton Wilder: American playwright and novelist. He won three Pulitzer Prizes for his novel The Bridge of San Luis Rey and for the plays Our Town and The Skin of Our Teeth. He was awarded a U.S. National Book Award for the novel The Eighth Day.

Art Williams: Business advisor and life coach.

Marianne Williamson: American author, spiritual leader, and political activist. She has written 13 books, including four New York Times number one bestsellers.

Oprah Winfrey: American talk show host, television producer, actress, author and philanthropist.

William Wordsworth: English Romantic poet who, with Samuel Taylor Coleridge, helped to launch the Romantic Age in English literature with their joint publication Lyrical Ballads.

Mike Yaconelli: Writer, theologian, church leader and satirist. Co-Founder of Youth Specialties, a training organization for Christian youth leaders, and The Wittenburg Door, a satirical magazine.

Paramahansa Yogananda: Indian Hindu monk, yogi and guru who introduced millions to the teachings of meditation and Kriya Yoga through his organization Self-Realization Fellowship/Yogoda Satsanga Society of India. He is the author of "Autobiography of a Yogi", which was designated one of the "100 Most Important Spiritual Books of the 20th Century.

Maharishi Mahesh Yogi: Indian yoga guru, known for developing and popularizing Transcendental Meditation(™), and for being the leader and guru of a worldwide organization.

Dogen Zenji: Zen master, also known as Dōgen Kigen, Eihei Dōgen, Kōso Jōyō Daishi, or Busshō Dentō Kokushi, was a Japanese Buddhist priest, writer, poet, philosopher, and founder of the Sōtō school of Zen in Japan.

* Biographies of people quoted were found either on author, personality, or organization websites, as well as at the Wikipedia Biography Portal:
https://en.wikipedia.org/wiki/Portal:Biography

Made in United States
North Haven, CT
26 October 2022

25959520R00141